THE PHILOSOPHY OF CHAPLAINCY

Dr. Maxwell Shimba

Printed by Shimba Publishing LLC
Printed in the United States of America

TABLE OF CONTENTS

INTRODUCTION

The Essence and Significance of Chaplaincy

The Essence of Chaplaincy

Chaplaincy is more than just a job; it is a calling, a vocation that requires deep empathy, unwavering faith, and a commitment to serving others. At its core, chaplaincy is about providing spiritual guidance, emotional support, and ethical counseling to individuals across a wide range of contexts. Whether in the quiet halls of a hospital, the bustling corridors of a university, the structured environment of a correctional facility, the regimented life of the military, or the dynamic atmosphere of a corporate office, chaplains bring a sense of calm, understanding, and hope.

The Philosophy Underlying Chaplaincy

The philosophy of chaplaincy is rooted in the belief that every individual has inherent worth and dignity and that spiritual well-being is an integral part of overall health. Chaplains operate on the principle that spiritual care is a crucial component of holistic care, addressing not only the mind and body but also the soul. This holistic approach recognizes that spiritual, emotional, and ethical dimensions are interconnected and essential for a person's well-being.

Chaplaincy is also characterized by its inclusivity and adaptability. Chaplains serve people of all faiths and none, respecting and honoring diverse beliefs and practices. This inclusivity is a cornerstone of chaplaincy, enabling chaplains to provide meaningful support to everyone they encounter, regardless of their background.

The Role of Chaplains in Different Settings

Military Chaplaincy: Military chaplains play a crucial role in supporting the spiritual and emotional needs of service members. They provide counseling, lead religious services, and offer a comforting presence in times of conflict and peace. Military chaplains often face unique challenges, such as ethical dilemmas in combat situations and the need to support individuals dealing with trauma and loss.

Healthcare Chaplaincy: In healthcare settings, chaplains provide essential support to patients, families, and staff. They offer comfort and guidance during difficult diagnoses, end-of-life care, and recovery. Healthcare chaplains help individuals find meaning and hope amidst illness and suffering, contributing to holistic patient care.

Corporate Chaplaincy: Corporate chaplains address the spiritual and emotional needs of employees in the workplace. They provide support during personal and professional challenges, promote ethical behavior, and foster a positive corporate culture. In an increasingly stressful work environment, corporate chaplains help employees find balance and purpose.

Educational Chaplaincy: Educational chaplains serve in schools, colleges, and universities, supporting students, faculty, and staff. They address the spiritual and emotional needs of young people navigating academic pressures and personal growth. Educational chaplains also contribute to creating inclusive and supportive campus environments.

Correctional Chaplaincy: Chaplains in correctional facilities provide spiritual care and guidance to inmates. They support rehabilitation and personal transformation, offering hope and a path to redemption. Correctional chaplains face the challenge of addressing the diverse spiritual needs of inmates in a structured and often challenging environment.

Ethical and Theological Foundations

The ethical and theological foundations of chaplaincy are deeply intertwined. Chaplains operate within a framework of ethical principles, such as confidentiality, respect for autonomy, and cultural competence. These principles guide their interactions and ensure that they provide care that is respectful and compassionate.

Theologically, chaplaincy is grounded in the teachings of various religious traditions that emphasize the importance of caring for others. Chaplains draw on these teachings to provide spiritual guidance and support, helping individuals connect with their faith and find meaning in their experiences.

The Purpose of This Book

This book aims to provide a comprehensive exploration of the philosophy of chaplaincy. By delving into its history, core principles, and diverse applications, we hope to offer insights into the unique role of chaplains in various settings. We will examine the challenges and opportunities that chaplains face, the ethical and theological foundations of their practice, and the impact of their work on individuals and communities.

Through this exploration, we aim to highlight the profound significance of chaplaincy and its enduring relevance in modern society. Whether you are a current or aspiring chaplain, a professional in a related field, or simply interested in understanding more about this vital vocation, we hope this book will provide valuable knowledge and inspiration.

Structure of the Book

The book is organized into ten chapters, each focusing on a specific aspect of chaplaincy. We begin with a historical overview of chaplaincy, tracing its origins and evolution. We then explore the core principles and theological foundations that underpin chaplaincy practice. Subsequent chapters delve into the role of chaplains in different settings, including military, healthcare, corporate, educational, and correctional institutions.

We also address the ethical framework of chaplaincy, examining the principles that guide chaplains in their practice. Finally, we look to the future, considering emerging trends and the ongoing evolution of chaplaincy in a rapidly changing world.

By the end of this book, we hope you will have a deeper understanding of the philosophy of chaplaincy and its vital role in providing spiritual, emotional, and ethical support across various contexts.

DR. MAXWELL SHIMBA

CHAPTER 01

THE ORIGINS AND EVOLUTION OF CHAPLAINCY

Ancient and Medieval Roots: The Historical Origins of Chaplaincy

The role of the chaplain has a rich and varied history that stretches back thousands of years. The concept of providing spiritual care to individuals in need is deeply embedded in the fabric of human society, and this chapter will explore the origins and evolution of chaplaincy from its ancient roots to the medieval period.

Ancient Roots of Chaplaincy

The earliest forms of chaplaincy can be traced back to ancient civilizations where religious leaders served as spiritual guides and counselors to warriors, leaders, and communities. These early chaplains were often priests, shamans, or other religious figures who provided spiritual support, conducted rituals, and offered counsel in times of war and peace.

Ancient Egypt: In ancient Egypt, priests played a crucial role in both religious and social life. They were responsible for maintaining the spiritual well-being of the community, conducting rituals, and providing guidance to rulers and warriors. Temples were not only places of worship but also centers of learning and healing, where priests acted as spiritual caregivers.

Ancient Greece and Rome: In ancient Greece and Rome, religious leaders known as augurs and pontiffs provided spiritual counsel to military leaders and citizens. These religious figures performed rituals to seek divine favor and guidance before battles, and they were integral to maintaining the moral and spiritual order of society. The presence of these spiritual advisors highlights the importance of religious support in ancient military and civic life.

Hebrew Tradition: The Hebrew Bible (Old Testament) contains numerous references to priests and prophets who provided spiritual care to the people of Israel. Figures such as Samuel, who anointed kings and offered counsel, and the Levitical priests, who performed sacrifices and rituals, can be seen as early examples of chaplaincy. Their role was to maintain the covenant between God and the people, offering spiritual guidance and support.

Early Christian Chaplaincy

With the rise of Christianity, the concept of chaplaincy began to take on more formalized and structured forms. Early Christian leaders recognized the need for spiritual care and support, particularly in times of persecution and conflict.

The Roman Empire: During the early years of Christianity, bishops and priests often accompanied Roman soldiers into battle, providing spiritual support and administering sacraments. One of the most notable early Christian chaplains was Saint Martin of Tours, a Roman soldier who converted to Christianity and later became a bishop. Saint Martin is traditionally regarded as the patron saint of chaplains, symbolizing the integration of military and spiritual life.

Monastic Communities: The rise of monasticism in the early centuries of Christianity also contributed to the development of chaplaincy. Monastic communities, such as those founded by Saint Benedict, emphasized the importance of prayer, contemplation, and service. Monks often served as spiritual advisors to both laypeople and leaders, offering guidance and support.

Medieval Chaplaincy

The medieval period saw the formalization and expansion of chaplaincy roles, particularly within the context of the Christian Church. Chaplains became more organized and their duties more clearly defined, as they served in various capacities within both religious and secular institutions.

Crusades and Military Orders: The Crusades (11th to 13th centuries) were a significant period for the development of military chaplaincy. Chaplains accompanied crusading armies, providing spiritual care to knights and soldiers. Military orders such as the Knights Templar and the Knights Hospitaller included chaplains who were responsible for the spiritual well-being of their members. These chaplains conducted religious services, offered confession, and provided moral support in the midst of battle.

Royal and Noble Courts: During the medieval period, chaplains also served in the courts of kings and nobles. These court chaplains provided spiritual guidance to rulers and their families, conducted religious ceremonies, and often served as advisors on matters of ethics and morality. The presence of chaplains in royal courts underscored the close relationship between the church and the state.

Cathedrals and Parish Churches: The medieval Church was a central institution in European society, and chaplains played a crucial role in its functioning. Cathedral chaplains assisted bishops in their duties, conducted daily services, and provided pastoral care to the community. In parish churches, chaplains supported the parish priest, helping to meet the spiritual needs of the local population.

Hospitals and Almonries: The medieval period also saw the establishment of hospitals and almonries (charitable institutions), where chaplains provided spiritual care to the sick, the poor, and the dying. These chaplains were responsible for administering the sacraments, offering prayers, and providing comfort to those in need. The role of chaplains in these institutions highlighted the importance of spiritual care in the medieval understanding of health and well-being.

Key Figures in Medieval Chaplaincy

Several key figures from the medieval period exemplify the role and importance of chaplaincy:

Saint Francis of Assisi: Known for his devotion to poverty and service, Saint Francis founded the Franciscan Order, which emphasized the importance of ministering to the poor and marginalized. Franciscan friars often served as chaplains in various capacities, bringing spiritual care to those in need.

Saint Bernard of Clairvaux: A prominent Cistercian monk, Saint Bernard played a significant role in the spiritual and political life of medieval Europe. He was a counselor to popes and kings and provided spiritual guidance during the

Second Crusade. His writings and teachings influenced the development of medieval spirituality and chaplaincy.

Julian of Norwich: An anchorite and mystic, Julian of Norwich provided spiritual counsel and guidance through her writings and her life of prayer and contemplation. Her work, "Revelations of Divine Love," remains a significant contribution to Christian spirituality and chaplaincy.

The Legacy of Ancient and Medieval Chaplaincy

The ancient and medieval roots of chaplaincy laid the foundation for the diverse and multifaceted vocation that we recognize today. The early chaplains, whether priests, monks, or religious leaders, established the principles of spiritual care, ethical guidance, and compassionate service that continue to guide chaplaincy practice.

These early forms of chaplaincy demonstrated the importance of providing spiritual support in times of conflict, illness, and personal crisis. They also highlighted the vital role of chaplains in maintaining the moral and spiritual fabric of society, offering a model of service that has endured through the centuries.

Development Through the Ages: How Chaplaincy Evolved Through the Middle Ages and the Reformation

The evolution of chaplaincy from the Middle Ages through the Reformation marked significant developments in the role and function of chaplains. As society changed, so too did the needs and expectations of spiritual care. This chapter explores how chaplaincy adapted to these changing societal needs, reflecting broader religious, cultural, and social transformations.

Chaplaincy in the High Middle Ages

The High Middle Ages (11th to 13th centuries) was a period of significant growth and consolidation for the Christian Church. This era saw the formalization of chaplaincy roles and the expansion of their duties in various institutions.

Military Chaplaincy During the Crusades: The Crusades profoundly influenced the development of military chaplaincy. Chaplains accompanied crusading armies to the Holy Land, providing spiritual support, conducting religious services, and offering pastoral care to soldiers. Military orders, such as the Knights Templar and the Knights Hospitaller, included chaplains who played crucial roles in maintaining the spiritual well-being of their members. These chaplains not only led prayers and administered sacraments but also offered moral support during battles and sieges.

Royal and Noble Courts: Chaplains became increasingly important in the courts of kings and nobles, where they served as spiritual advisors, conducted religious ceremonies, and provided ethical guidance. Their presence in royal courts underscored the interweaving of religious and political life during this period. Court chaplains often acted as confidants to rulers, influencing decisions on matters of state and morality.

Cathedrals and Monastic Communities: The medieval Church's influence extended through cathedrals and monastic communities, where chaplains played vital roles. Cathedral chaplains assisted bishops in liturgical duties, managed church affairs, and provided pastoral care. Monastic chaplains supported the spiritual and communal life of monks, facilitating prayer, meditation, and service. Monasteries often served as centers of learning and charity, with chaplains helping to administer these functions.

Hospitals and Almonries: During the High Middle Ages, hospitals and almonries (charitable institutions) were established, reflecting the Church's commitment to caring for the sick and poor. Chaplains in these settings provided spiritual care, administered sacraments, and offered comfort to patients and the needy. These chaplains played a crucial role in the medieval understanding of holistic care, where physical healing was intertwined with spiritual well-being.

Late Middle Ages and the Dawn of the Reformation

The Late Middle Ages (14th to 15th centuries) were characterized by significant social, political, and religious upheaval. The Black Death, the Hundred Years' War, and the Great Schism profoundly affected European society and the Church, leading to changes in the role and perception of chaplains.

The Black Death: The devastating impact of the Black Death (1347-1351) led to an increased demand for chaplains to provide spiritual care to the dying and bereaved. Chaplains administered last rites, offered prayers, and provided comfort during a time of widespread fear and suffering. This period highlighted the critical role of chaplains in offering hope and spiritual solace amidst a crisis.

The Hundred Years' War: The prolonged conflict between England and France (1337-1453) saw chaplains continuing to serve military needs. They provided spiritual support to soldiers, conducted services, and maintained morale. The war emphasized the enduring importance of military chaplaincy in supporting the spiritual and emotional well-being of combatants.

The Great Schism: The Great Schism (1378-1417), which saw multiple claimants to the papacy, created significant turmoil within the Church. Chaplains navigated this complex religious landscape, often caught between competing allegiances. Despite the schism, chaplains remained dedicated to their pastoral duties, providing spiritual care and maintaining the faith of their communities.

The Reformation and Its Impact on Chaplaincy

The Reformation (16th century) brought profound changes to the Christian Church and the practice of chaplaincy. The movement, initiated by figures such as Martin Luther, John Calvin, and Huldrych Zwingli, sought to reform the Church's practices and doctrines, leading to the establishment of Protestantism.

Protestant Chaplaincy: The rise of Protestantism transformed chaplaincy in significant ways. Protestant chaplains focused on preaching, teaching, and pastoral care, emphasizing the importance of scripture and personal faith. The role of chaplains in Protestant communities often extended beyond traditional settings, reaching into homes and workplaces. Protestant chaplains played a crucial role in spreading Reformation ideas and supporting the spiritual growth of their congregations.

Military Chaplaincy: The Reformation era saw continued military conflicts, including the Wars of Religion in France and the Thirty Years' War in Central Europe. Protestant and Catholic chaplains served their respective armies, providing spiritual care, conducting services, and offering moral support. The presence of chaplains on both sides of these conflicts highlighted the deep religious divisions of the time.

Educational Institutions: The Reformation emphasized the importance of education and literacy, leading to the establishment of schools and universities. Chaplains in these institutions provided spiritual guidance, taught religious studies, and supported the moral development of students. The role of chaplains in education reflected the Reformation's focus on personal faith and understanding of scripture.

Healthcare and Social Services: Protestant reformers also emphasized the importance of caring for the sick and poor. Chaplains continued to serve in hospitals and charitable institutions, providing spiritual care and support. The Reformation's emphasis on personal responsibility and charity influenced the development of chaplaincy in these settings, promoting a holistic approach to care.

Key Figures in the Reformation and Chaplaincy

Several key figures from the Reformation era exemplify the evolving role of chaplaincy:

Martin Luther: As a seminal figure in the Reformation, Luther's emphasis on scripture and personal faith influenced Protestant chaplaincy. His writings and teachings shaped the spiritual care provided by Protestant chaplains, focusing on preaching, teaching, and pastoral support.

John Calvin: Calvin's emphasis on the sovereignty of God and the importance of community influenced the role of chaplains in Reformed traditions. Calvinist chaplains played a crucial role in supporting the spiritual and moral life of their congregations, emphasizing discipline and communal worship.

John Knox: A leading figure in the Scottish Reformation, Knox's emphasis on education and moral discipline influenced the role of chaplains in Scotland. Knox's work in establishing schools and promoting literacy highlighted the educational aspect of chaplaincy.

The Legacy of the Middle Ages and Reformation

The development of chaplaincy through the Middle Ages and the Reformation laid the groundwork for modern chaplaincy practice. The formalization of chaplaincy roles, the expansion of their duties, and the adaptation to changing societal needs demonstrated the resilience and flexibility of this vocation.

The evolution of chaplaincy during these periods reflected broader religious, cultural, and social transformations. Chaplains played a critical role in supporting the spiritual and emotional well-being of individuals and communities, offering care and guidance in times of conflict, crisis, and change.

As we move forward in this book, we will explore how these historical developments continued to shape chaplaincy in the modern era, examining the ongoing relevance and impact of chaplains in various contemporary settings. The legacy of the Middle Ages and the Reformation provides a rich historical context that helps us understand the enduring significance of chaplaincy as a unique and vital vocation.

Modern Chaplaincy: The Transformation of Chaplaincy in the 19th and 20th Centuries

The 19th and 20th centuries were pivotal periods for the transformation and formalization of chaplaincy. During this time, chaplaincy evolved to meet the changing needs of society, adapting to new contexts and expanding its roles and functions. This chapter explores the significant developments in chaplaincy during these centuries, highlighting the key changes and innovations that shaped modern chaplaincy practice.

The 19th Century: Formalization and Expansion

The 19th century witnessed significant social, political, and technological changes that influenced the development of chaplaincy. The Industrial Revolution, the rise of nation-states, and the expansion of colonial empires created new contexts and challenges for chaplains.

Military Chaplaincy: The 19th century saw the formalization of military chaplaincy in many nations. As standing armies became more common, the need for structured spiritual support for soldiers grew. Military chaplains were officially integrated into armed forces, providing religious services, pastoral care, and moral guidance. The establishment of formal chaplaincy corps, such as the British Army Chaplains' Department (established in 1796), exemplified this trend. Chaplains accompanied troops during conflicts such as the Napoleonic Wars, the Crimean War, and the American Civil War, offering vital support to soldiers.

Healthcare Chaplaincy: The development of modern hospitals during the 19th century created new opportunities for chaplaincy. Chaplains were appointed to hospitals to provide spiritual care to patients, families, and staff. The role of healthcare chaplains expanded to include pastoral counseling, sacramental ministry, and end-of-life care. Florence Nightingale, a pioneering figure in modern nursing, emphasized the importance of holistic care, including spiritual support, in her work.

Prison Chaplaincy: The reform movement of the 19th century led to significant changes in the penal system, century led to significant changes in the penal system, including the introduction of prison chaplains. Chaplains were appointed to provide spiritual care, moral guidance, and support for the rehabilitation of inmates. The work of prison chaplains emphasized the potential for personal transformation and redemption, aligning with broader humanitarian and reformist ideals of the period.

Educational Institutions: The expansion of public education in the 19th century also influenced chaplaincy. Chaplains were appointed to schools, colleges, and universities to provide spiritual and moral guidance to students. They played a crucial role in the moral and ethical development of young people, offering support and counseling in academic settings.

The Early 20th Century: Professionalization and Diversification

The early 20th century brought further professionalization and diversification of chaplaincy roles. The two World Wars, the Great Depression, and significant social changes influenced the evolution of chaplaincy in various contexts.

World War 1 and II: The two World Wars had a profound impact on military chaplaincy. The scale and intensity of these conflicts highlighted the need for comprehensive spiritual and emotional support for soldiers.

Military chaplains provided religious services, counseling, and comfort to troops on the front lines and in military hospitals. They also played a key role in supporting the families of service members. The experiences of military chaplains during these wars led to increased recognition of their contributions and the formalization of their roles within armed forces.

Healthcare Chaplaincy: The early 20th century saw significant advancements in medical science and the expansion of healthcare institutions. Healthcare chaplaincy continued to evolve, with chaplains becoming integral members of multidisciplinary healthcare teams. They provided spiritual care, pastoral counseling, and support for patients facing serious illnesses and end-of-life issues. The establishment of professional associations, such as the Association of Professional Chaplains (founded in 1946), contributed to the professionalization of healthcare chaplaincy.

Corporate Chaplaincy: The rise of large corporations and industrial enterprises in the early 20th century created new opportunities for chaplaincy. Corporate chaplains were appointed to provide spiritual and emotional support to employees, promote ethical behavior, and foster a positive workplace culture. The work of corporate chaplains reflected the growing recognition of the importance of employee well-being and the role of spirituality in the workplace.

Educational and Campus Chaplaincy: The expansion of higher education in the early 20th century led to the formalization of chaplaincy roles in colleges and universities. Campus chaplains provided spiritual guidance, counseling, and support for students navigating academic pressures and personal growth. They also played a key role in fostering inclusive and supportive campus communities, addressing issues related to diversity and social justice.

The Mid to Late 20th Century: Institutionalization and Integration

The mid to late 20th century saw the further institutionalization and integration of chaplaincy into various sectors of society. This period was marked by significant social, cultural, and technological changes that influenced the practice of chaplaincy.

Civil Rights Movement: The Civil Rights Movement of the 1950s and 1960s had a profound impact on chaplaincy, particularly in the United States. Many chaplains were actively involved in advocating for social justice, equality, and human rights. Their work highlighted the intersection of faith, ethics, and social action, and emphasized the role of chaplaincy in addressing systemic injustices and promoting social change.

Healthcare Chaplaincy: The latter half of the 20th century saw significant advancements in healthcare chaplaincy, including the development of clinical pastoral education (CPE) programs. CPE programs provided structured training and supervision for chaplains, emphasizing the importance of professional competence, self-awareness, and reflective practice. The integration of chaplaincy into multidisciplinary healthcare teams became more formalized, with chaplains contributing to holistic patient care.

Military Chaplaincy: The Vietnam War and subsequent conflicts continued to shape military chaplaincy. The experiences of chaplains in these conflicts highlighted the importance of addressing the spiritual and emotional needs of service members dealing with trauma, moral injury, and post-traumatic stress disorder (PTSD). The role of military chaplains expanded to include providing support for veterans and their families.

Corporate and Workplace Chaplaincy: The growth of the global economy and the increasing complexity of the workplace led to the expansion of corporate chaplaincy. Chaplains provided support for employees facing personal and professional challenges, promoted ethical leadership, and contributed to creating positive workplace environments. The work of corporate chaplains reflected the growing recognition of the importance of mental health and well-being in the workplace.

Educational Chaplaincy: The mid to late 20th century saw the continued evolution of educational chaplaincy. Campus chaplains played a crucial role in supporting students' spiritual and emotional well-being, promoting interfaith dialogue, and addressing issues related to diversity and inclusion. The work of educational chaplains reflected the changing landscape of higher education and the increasing diversity of student populations.

Key Figures in Modern Chaplaincy

Several key figures from the 19th and 20th centuries exemplify the transformation and professionalization of chaplaincy:

William Booth: The founder of the Salvation Army, Booth emphasized the importance of providing spiritual and practical support to marginalized and vulnerable populations. His work highlighted the role of chaplaincy in addressing social issues and promoting holistic care.

Anton Boisen: A pioneer in the field of clinical pastoral education, Boisen's work emphasized the importance of professional training and reflective practice for chaplains. His contributions to healthcare chaplaincy have had a lasting impact on the field.

Martin Luther King Jr.: As a leader of the Civil Rights Movement and a Baptist minister, King exemplified the intersection of faith, ethics, and social action. His work highlighted the role of chaplaincy in advocating for justice and promoting social change.

The Legacy of Modern Chaplaincy

The transformation of chaplaincy in the 19th and 20th centuries laid the foundation for the diverse and professionalized chaplaincy practice we recognize today. The formalization of chaplaincy roles, the integration into various institutions, and the emphasis on professional competence and ethical practice have shaped modern chaplaincy into a vital and dynamic vocation.

The developments during these centuries reflected broader social, cultural, and technological changes, highlighting the adaptability and resilience of chaplaincy in meeting the evolving needs of society. As we move forward in this book, we will explore the continued evolution of chaplaincy in the 21st century, examining the ongoing relevance and impact of chaplains in various contemporary settings.

CHAPTER 02

CORE PRINCIPLES OF CHAPLAINCY

Spiritual Care: The Centrality of Providing Spiritual Support and Fostering Spiritual Well-Being

Spiritual care is at the heart of chaplaincy, serving as the foundation upon which the vocation is built. This chapter delves into the nature of spiritual care, its importance, and the various ways chaplains provide this essential support. By exploring the dimensions of spiritual care, we aim to understand how chaplains foster spiritual well-being across different contexts and faith traditions.

Understanding Spiritual Care

Defining Spiritual Care: Spiritual care involves addressing the spiritual needs of individuals, which may include their sense of purpose, connection to the divine, moral and ethical beliefs, and their experience of suffering and joy. It is a holistic approach that recognizes the interconnectedness of mind, body, and spirit.

The Importance of Spiritual Care: Spiritual care is crucial for overall well-being. It helps individuals find meaning and purpose, cope with life's challenges, and experience a sense of peace and fulfillment. By addressing spiritual needs, chaplains contribute to the holistic care of individuals, complementing physical and emotional support.

The Role of Chaplains in Providing Spiritual Care

Listening and Presence: One of the fundamental aspects of spiritual care is active listening. Chaplains provide a compassionate and non-judgmental presence, allowing individuals to express their thoughts, feelings, and spiritual concerns. This presence fosters trust and creates a safe space for individuals to explore their spirituality.

Prayer and Meditation: Prayer and meditation are central practices in many religious traditions. Chaplains lead prayers, guide meditations, and offer spiritual practices that align with the individual's faith or spiritual background. These practices provide comfort, solace, and a means of connecting with the divine.

Sacramental Ministry: In religious traditions that observe sacraments, chaplains administer these rites as part of their spiritual care. Sacraments such as baptism, communion, anointing of the sick, and confession play a significant role in the spiritual life of individuals and communities, offering spiritual nourishment and healing.

Rituals and Ceremonies: Rituals and ceremonies mark significant moments in life, such as births, marriages, and deaths. Chaplains conduct these rituals, providing spiritual support during these transitions. Rituals offer a sense of continuity, meaning, and community connection, helping individuals navigate life's changes.

Spiritual Counseling: Chaplains provide spiritual counseling, offering guidance and support as individuals grapple with existential questions, moral dilemmas, and spiritual crises. Through counseling, chaplains help individuals find clarity, make ethical decisions, and strengthen their spiritual resilience.

The Dimensions of Spiritual Care

Holistic Approach: Spiritual care is holistic, addressing the physical, emotional, and spiritual aspects of well-being. Chaplains work alongside healthcare professionals, social workers, and counselors to provide integrated care that meets the comprehensive needs of individuals.

Interfaith and Multifaith Care: In diverse settings, chaplains often serve individuals from various religious and spiritual backgrounds. Interfaith and multifaith care involve respecting and honoring different beliefs, practices, and traditions. Chaplains provide inclusive spiritual care, ensuring that everyone receives meaningful support regardless of their faith.

Cultural Competence: Cultural competence is essential in providing effective spiritual care. Chaplains must understand and respect cultural differences, recognizing how culture influences spiritual beliefs and practices. Culturally competent care fosters trust and ensures that spiritual support is relevant and respectful.

Ethical Considerations: Ethical principles guide the practice of spiritual care. Confidentiality, respect for autonomy, and informed consent are critical components. Chaplains must navigate ethical dilemmas with sensitivity, ensuring that their care aligns with the values and wishes of the individuals they serve.

The Impact of Spiritual Care

Emotional and Psychological Well-Being: Spiritual care positively impacts emotional and psychological well-being. It provides individuals with coping mechanisms, reduces anxiety and depression, and enhances resilience. The support of a chaplain can lead to improved mental health outcomes.

Sense of Community and Belonging: Spiritual care fosters a sense of community and belonging. Chaplains help individuals connect with their faith communities, creating networks of support. This sense of belonging is particularly important in times of crisis and isolation.

End-of-Life Care: At the end of life, spiritual care is vital in providing comfort, peace, and meaning. Chaplains support individuals and their families through the dying process, offering prayers, rituals, and presence. Spiritual care at this stage helps individuals find closure and transition with dignity.

Moral and Ethical Decision-Making: Spiritual care supports individuals in making moral and ethical decisions. Chaplains offer guidance rooted in spiritual and ethical principles, helping individuals navigate complex choices with integrity and clarity.

Case Studies in Spiritual Care

Healthcare Chaplaincy: In a hospital setting, a chaplain provides spiritual care to a terminally ill patient and their family. Through prayers, listening, and administering the sacraments, the chaplain helps the patient find peace and the family find solace.

Military Chaplaincy: A military chaplain supports soldiers in a conflict zone, offering spiritual care through counseling, leading worship services, and providing a comforting presence. The chaplain's support helps soldiers cope with the stresses of combat and maintain their morale.

Corporate Chaplaincy: In a corporate environment, a chaplain assists an employee dealing with personal and professional challenges. Through spiritual counseling and support, the chaplain helps the employee find balance, purpose, and improved well-being.

Educational Chaplaincy: A campus chaplain supports a student struggling with academic pressures and personal issues. The chaplain offers a listening ear, spiritual guidance, and resources for coping, helping the student navigate their challenges and find spiritual strength.

Challenges and Opportunities in Spiritual Care

Secularization and Pluralism: The increasing secularization and religious pluralism of society present challenges for chaplains in providing spiritual care. Chaplains must navigate these complexities, finding ways to offer meaningful support that respects diverse beliefs and values.

Training and Professional Development: Continuous training and professional development are essential for chaplains to provide effective spiritual care. Programs in clinical pastoral education and ongoing professional development opportunities equip chaplains with the skills and knowledge needed to meet the evolving needs of those they serve.

Integration into Multidisciplinary Teams: The integration of chaplains into multidisciplinary teams enhances the provision of holistic care. Collaborative approaches ensure that spiritual care is an integral part of overall well-being, addressing the comprehensive needs of individuals.

Innovations in Spiritual Care: Innovations in spiritual care, such as the use of technology and telechaplaincy, offer new opportunities for reaching and supporting individuals. These advancements enable chaplains to provide care in diverse and remote settings, expanding their impact.

Spiritual care is the cornerstone of chaplaincy, embodying the essence of the vocation. By providing spiritual support and fostering spiritual well-being, chaplains play a vital role in the holistic care of individuals across various contexts. The dimensions of spiritual care—listening and presence, prayer and meditation, sacramental ministry, rituals and ceremonies, and spiritual counseling—highlight the multifaceted nature of this support.

Emotional and Psychological Support: Addressing the Emotional and Mental Health Needs of Individuals

While spiritual care forms the heart of chaplaincy, addressing the emotional and psychological well-being of individuals is equally vital. Chaplains play a crucial role in supporting mental health, providing compassionate presence, counseling, and guidance in various settings. This chapter explores the importance of emotional and psychological support in chaplaincy, examining the methods and approaches chaplains use to meet these needs.

Understanding Emotional and Psychological Support

Defining Emotional and Psychological Support: Emotional and psychological support involves helping individuals manage their emotions, cope with stress, and navigate mental health challenges. This support encompasses listening, empathy, counseling, and providing resources for mental well-being.

The Importance of Emotional and Psychological Support: Emotional and psychological health is essential for overall well-being. Addressing these needs helps individuals cope with life's difficulties, build resilience, and improve their quality of life. Chaplains play a key role in fostering emotional and psychological health, complementing other forms of care.

The Role of Chaplains in Providing Emotional and Psychological Support

Active Listening and Empathy: One of the primary ways chaplains provide emotional support is through active listening and empathy. By offering a non-judgmental and compassionate presence, chaplains allow individuals to express their feelings and concerns. This process helps individuals feel heard, understood, and validated.

Counseling and Guidance: Chaplains provide counseling to help individuals navigate emotional and psychological challenges. This counseling can address a wide range of issues, including grief, anxiety, depression, relationship problems, and moral dilemmas. Chaplains offer guidance rooted in compassion and ethical principles, helping individuals find clarity and direction.

Crisis Intervention: In times of crisis, chaplains offer immediate emotional and psychological support. Whether dealing with trauma, sudden loss, or acute mental health issues, chaplains provide a calming presence and practical assistance. They help individuals stabilize, process their experiences, and access additional resources if needed.

Support Groups and Peer Support: Chaplains often facilitate support groups, providing a space for individuals to share their experiences and receive mutual support. These groups can address specific issues, such as bereavement, addiction recovery, or stress management. Chaplains guide these groups, fostering a supportive and empathetic environment.

Mindfulness and Stress Reduction Techniques: Chaplains incorporate mindfulness and stress reduction techniques into their support strategies. Practices such as deep breathing, meditation, and relaxation exercises help individuals manage stress, reduce anxiety, and enhance emotional well-being.

The Dimensions of Emotional and Psychological Support

Holistic Approach: Emotional and psychological support in chaplaincy is holistic, addressing the interconnectedness of mind, body, and spirit. Chaplains recognize that emotional health impacts physical and spiritual well-being, and they work collaboratively with other healthcare professionals to provide comprehensive care.

Interfaith and Multicultural Sensitivity: Chaplains serve individuals from diverse religious, cultural, and ethnic backgrounds. Providing emotional and psychological support requires sensitivity to these differences, ensuring that care is respectful and relevant. Chaplains must understand and honor various cultural expressions of emotion and coping mechanisms.

Ethical Considerations: Ethical principles are fundamental to providing emotional and psychological support. Chaplains must maintain confidentiality, respect autonomy, and obtain informed consent. Navigating ethical dilemmas with sensitivity and integrity ensures that individuals receive care that aligns with their values and wishes.

Building Resilience: One of the goals of emotional and psychological support is to help individuals build resilience. Chaplains assist individuals in developing coping strategies, enhancing their ability to manage stress and adversity. By fostering resilience, chaplains contribute to long-term emotional health and well-being.

The Impact of Emotional and Psychological Support

Improved Mental Health Outcomes: Emotional and psychological support from chaplains leads to improved mental health outcomes. Individuals experience reduced symptoms of anxiety and depression, enhanced coping skills, and greater emotional stability. The presence of a chaplain can significantly impact an individual's journey towards mental health recovery.

Enhanced Coping Mechanisms: Chaplains help individuals develop and strengthen their coping mechanisms. Whether through counseling, support groups, or mindfulness practices, chaplains provide tools that individuals can use to manage stress and emotional challenges effectively.

Sense of Connection and Belonging: Emotional and psychological support fosters a sense of connection and belonging. Chaplains help individuals feel part of a supportive community, reducing feelings of isolation and loneliness. This sense of connection is particularly important in times of crisis or transition.

Holistic Well-Being: By addressing emotional and psychological needs, chaplains contribute to holistic well-being. Individuals experience improved physical health, spiritual fulfillment, and overall life satisfaction. The integration of emotional support into holistic care enhances the quality of life for those served.

Case Studies in Emotional and Psychological Support

Healthcare Chaplaincy: In a hospital, a chaplain supports a patient diagnosed with a chronic illness. Through regular visits, active listening, and counseling, the chaplain helps the patient manage anxiety, navigate treatment decisions, and find hope amidst their health challenges.

Military Chaplaincy: A military chaplain assists a soldier returning from deployment who is struggling with post-traumatic stress disorder (PTSD). The chaplain provides counseling, facilitates support groups, and introduces mindfulness techniques, helping the soldier build resilience and reconnect with their sense of purpose.

Corporate Chaplaincy: In a corporate setting, a chaplain supports an employee experiencing workplace stress and burnout. Through one-on-one counseling and stress reduction workshops, the chaplain helps the employee develop coping strategies, improve work-life balance, and enhance their overall well-being.

Educational Chaplaincy: A campus chaplain supports a student facing academic pressures and personal issues. The chaplain provides a safe space for the student to express their concerns, offers emotional support, and connects the student with additional campus resources. This support helps the student navigate their challenges and achieve academic success.

Challenges and Opportunities in Emotional and Psychological Support

Stigma Around Mental Health: One of the challenges in providing emotional and psychological support is the stigma surrounding mental health issues. Chaplains play a crucial role in normalizing discussions about mental health and encouraging individuals to seek help. By addressing stigma, chaplains create a more accepting and supportive environment.

Training and Professional Development: Continuous training and professional development are essential for chaplains to provide effective emotional and psychological support. Programs in pastoral counseling, mental health first aid, and trauma-informed care equip chaplains with the skills needed to address complex emotional and psychological needs.

Collaboration with Mental Health Professionals: Collaboration with mental health professionals enhances the provision of emotional and psychological support. Chaplains work alongside psychologists, counselors, and social workers to provide comprehensive care. This interdisciplinary approach ensures that individuals receive the best possible support.

Innovations in Support Techniques: Innovations in support techniques, such as telechaplaincy and online counseling, offer new opportunities for reaching individuals in need. These advancements enable chaplains to provide emotional and psychological support in diverse and remote settings, expanding their impact.

Emotional and psychological support is a core principle of chaplaincy, reflecting the vocation's commitment to holistic care. By addressing the emotional and mental health needs of individuals, chaplains play a vital role in fostering overall well-being. The dimensions of emotional support—active listening, counseling, crisis intervention, support groups, and mindfulness—highlight the multifaceted nature of this care.

Ethical Guidance: The Role of Chaplains in Offering Ethical Counsel and Moral Support

Ethical guidance is a cornerstone of chaplaincy, reflecting the vocation's commitment to helping individuals navigate complex moral landscapes. Chaplains provide ethical counsel and moral support in various contexts, addressing dilemmas and fostering integrity. This chapter explores the role of chaplains in offering ethical guidance, examining the principles and practices that underpin this essential aspect of their work.

Understanding Ethical Guidance

Defining Ethical Guidance: Ethical guidance involves helping individuals make decisions that align with their values, beliefs, and moral principles. It encompasses counseling on ethical dilemmas, providing moral support, and fostering ethical reflection.

The Importance of Ethical Guidance: Ethical guidance is crucial for personal integrity and community well-being. It helps individuals resolve conflicts, make informed decisions, and act with moral clarity. Chaplains play a key role in promoting ethical behavior and supporting individuals in their moral development.

The Role of Chaplains in Providing Ethical Guidance

Counseling on Ethical Dilemmas: Chaplains often help individuals navigate ethical dilemmas, such as end-of-life decisions, professional ethics, and personal moral conflicts. Through counseling, chaplains provide a framework for ethical reflection, helping individuals weigh their options and consider the implications of their choices.

Moral Support: In addition to counseling, chaplains offer moral support to individuals facing difficult ethical decisions. This support includes listening, empathy, and encouragement, helping individuals feel confident and supported in their moral convictions.

Mediating Ethical Conflicts: Chaplains may also mediate ethical conflicts within families, organizations, or communities. By facilitating dialogue and promoting mutual understanding, chaplains help resolve conflicts and foster ethical harmony.

Promoting Ethical Reflection: Chaplains encourage ethical reflection through discussions, workshops, and educational programs. These activities help individuals and communities explore ethical issues, develop moral reasoning skills, and cultivate ethical awareness.

Supporting Organizational Ethics: In institutional settings, chaplains contribute to the development and implementation of ethical policies and practices. They provide ethical oversight, support ethical decision-making processes, and promote a culture of integrity.

The Dimensions of Ethical Guidance

Holistic Approach: Ethical guidance in chaplaincy is holistic, addressing the interconnectedness of ethical, spiritual, emotional, and social dimensions. Chaplains recognize that ethical decisions impact overall well-being and work to integrate ethical reflection into holistic care.

Interfaith and Multicultural Sensitivity: Chaplains serve individuals from diverse religious and cultural backgrounds. Providing ethical guidance requires sensitivity to different moral frameworks, ensuring that counsel is respectful and relevant. Chaplains must understand and honor various cultural expressions of ethics and morality.

Ethical Principles in Chaplaincy: Several ethical principles guide the practice of ethical guidance in chaplaincy:

- Autonomy: Respecting individuals' right to make their own decisions and supporting their capacity for self-determination.

- Confidentiality: Maintaining the privacy of individuals and ensuring that discussions remain confidential.

- Beneficence: Acting in the best interest of individuals, promoting their well-being and avoiding harm.

- Justice: Ensuring fairness and equity in ethical decision-making, addressing issues of rights and responsibilities.

Building Ethical Resilience: One of the goals of ethical guidance is to help individuals build ethical resilience. Chaplains assist individuals in developing the skills and confidence needed to navigate ethical challenges and maintain their moral integrity.

The Impact of Ethical Guidance

Enhanced Decision-Making: Ethical guidance from chaplains leads to enhanced decision-making. Individuals experience greater clarity, confidence, and moral alignment in their choices. The support of a chaplain can significantly impact an individual's ability to navigate complex ethical issues.

Moral Development: Ethical guidance fosters moral development, helping individuals refine their values, strengthen their moral reasoning, and cultivate ethical behavior. Chaplains play a key role in supporting individuals' moral growth and development.

Organizational Integrity: In institutional settings, chaplains contribute to organizational integrity by promoting ethical practices and supporting ethical decision-making processes. Their presence helps create a culture of ethical accountability and responsibility.

Community Cohesion: Ethical guidance fosters community cohesion by promoting mutual understanding, resolving conflicts, and supporting shared ethical values. Chaplains help build ethical communities where individuals feel supported and connected.

Case Studies in Ethical Guidance

Healthcare Chaplaincy: In a hospital, a chaplain supports a family facing end-of-life decisions for a loved one. Through counseling and ethical reflection, the chaplain helps the family consider their values, the patient's wishes, and medical options, leading to a compassionate and informed decision.

Military Chaplaincy: A military chaplain assists a soldier grappling with the ethical implications of combat. The chaplain provides moral support, helps the soldier reflect on their values, and offers guidance on navigating the ethical complexities of their role.

Corporate Chaplaincy: In a corporate setting, a chaplain supports an employee facing a professional ethical dilemma. Through one-on-one counseling and ethical reflection workshops, the chaplain helps the employee make decisions that align with their values and the company's ethical standards.

Educational Chaplaincy: A campus chaplain supports students discussing ethical issues in a classroom setting. The chaplain facilitates ethical reflection, encourages diverse perspectives, and helps students develop their moral reasoning skills.

Challenges and Opportunities in Ethical Guidance

Ethical Pluralism: One of the challenges in providing ethical guidance is navigating ethical pluralism—the coexistence of diverse moral frameworks. Chaplains must be adept at understanding and respecting different ethical perspectives while providing meaningful guidance.

Training and Professional Development: Continuous training and professional development are essential for chaplains to provide effective ethical guidance. Programs in ethics, moral theology, and ethical counseling equip chaplains with the skills needed to address complex ethical issues.

Collaboration with Ethics Committees: Collaboration with ethics committees and boards enhances the provision of ethical guidance. Chaplains work alongside ethicists, healthcare professionals, and organizational leaders to provide comprehensive ethical support.

Innovations in Ethical Guidance: Innovations in ethical guidance, such as the use of technology for remote counseling and ethical consultations, offer new opportunities for reaching individuals in need. These advancements enable chaplains to provide ethical guidance in diverse and remote settings, expanding their impact.

Ethical guidance is a core principle of chaplaincy, reflecting the vocation's commitment to helping individuals navigate complex moral landscapes. By providing ethical counsel and moral support, chaplains play a vital role in promoting ethical behavior, resolving conflicts, and fostering moral development. The dimensions of ethical guidance—counseling on ethical dilemmas, moral support, mediating conflicts, promoting ethical reflection, and supporting organizational ethics—highlight the multifaceted nature of this support.

Holistic Approach: Integrating Spiritual, Emotional, and Ethical Care into a Cohesive Practice

The holistic approach is a fundamental principle of chaplaincy, emphasizing the integration of spiritual, emotional, and ethical care into a unified practice. This chapter explores the concept of holistic care, its significance, and how chaplains implement this approach to address the comprehensive needs of individuals. By examining the dimensions and impact of holistic care, we aim to understand how chaplains foster overall well-being and harmony.

Understanding the Holistic Approach

Defining Holistic Care: Holistic care considers the whole person—body, mind, and spirit—recognizing that these dimensions are interconnected and influence each other. This approach aims to address the comprehensive needs of individuals, promoting overall well-being and balance.

The Importance of Holistic Care: Holistic care is crucial for fostering health and well-being. By addressing spiritual, emotional, and ethical needs, chaplains help individuals achieve a sense of harmony, purpose, and fulfillment. This integrated approach enhances the quality of care and supports long-term well-being.

The Role of Chaplains in Providing Holistic Care

Spiritual Care: Spiritual care is a core component of holistic chaplaincy. Chaplains provide spiritual support through practices such as prayer, meditation, sacramental ministry, and rituals. This care helps individuals connect with their faith, find meaning, and experience spiritual well-being.

Emotional and Psychological Support: Chaplains address emotional and psychological needs through active listening, counseling, crisis intervention, and support groups. By providing a compassionate presence and practical assistance, chaplains help individuals navigate emotional challenges, build resilience, and enhance mental health.

Ethical Guidance: Ethical guidance is integral to holistic care, helping individuals navigate moral dilemmas, make informed decisions, and act with integrity. Chaplains offer ethical counsel, moral support, and facilitate ethical reflection, fostering ethical awareness and moral development.

Interdisciplinary Collaboration: Chaplains often collaborate with other healthcare professionals, social workers, and counselors to provide comprehensive care. This interdisciplinary approach ensures that all aspects of an individual's well-being are addressed, promoting holistic health.

The Dimensions of Holistic Care

Holistic Assessment: Holistic care begins with a comprehensive assessment of an individual's spiritual, emotional, and ethical needs. Chaplains gather information through discussions, observations, and collaboration with other professionals to develop a complete understanding of the individual's situation.

Integrated Care Plans: Chaplains create integrated care plans that address the spiritual, emotional, and ethical dimensions of well-being. These plans include specific interventions, practices, and resources tailored to the individual's needs, promoting cohesive and coordinated care.

Cultural Competence: Providing holistic care requires cultural competence, recognizing and respecting diverse cultural, religious, and ethical backgrounds. Chaplains ensure that care is relevant, respectful, and sensitive to individual beliefs and practices.

Ongoing Evaluation: Holistic care involves ongoing evaluation and adjustment of care plans to meet changing needs. Chaplains regularly assess the effectiveness of interventions, gather feedback, and make necessary modifications to ensure continuous and comprehensive support.

The Impact of Holistic Care

Enhanced Well-Being: Holistic care leads to enhanced overall well-being by addressing the interconnected dimensions of an individual's life. Individuals experience improved spiritual fulfillment, emotional stability, and ethical clarity, contributing to a balanced and harmonious life.

Improved Health Outcomes: Integrating spiritual, emotional, and ethical care into a cohesive practice leads to improved health outcomes. Holistic care reduces stress, enhances coping mechanisms, and promotes physical health by addressing the root causes of emotional and psychological distress.

Strengthened Resilience: Holistic care builds resilience by providing individuals with the tools and support needed to navigate life's challenges. Chaplains help individuals develop coping strategies, strengthen their spiritual and ethical foundations, and enhance their ability to adapt and thrive.

Increased Satisfaction and Trust: Individuals receiving holistic care report higher levels of satisfaction and trust in their care providers. The comprehensive and compassionate nature of holistic care fosters a strong therapeutic relationship, enhancing the overall care experience.

Case Studies in Holistic Care

Healthcare Chaplaincy: In a hospital, a chaplain provides holistic care to a patient recovering from surgery. The chaplain offers spiritual support through prayer, emotional support through counseling, and ethical guidance in making post-surgery lifestyle changes. The integrated care plan helps the patient achieve physical recovery, emotional stability, and spiritual well-being.

Military Chaplaincy: A military chaplain supports a soldier returning from deployment. The chaplain addresses the soldier's spiritual needs through religious services, emotional needs through counseling for PTSD, and ethical needs by helping the soldier navigate moral injuries. The holistic approach fosters the soldier's overall recovery and reintegration into civilian life.

Corporate Chaplaincy: In a corporate setting, a chaplain provides holistic care to an employee facing personal and professional challenges. The chaplain offers spiritual practices such as mindfulness, emotional support through stress management workshops, and ethical guidance in navigating workplace dilemmas. The integrated care plan enhances the employee's well-being and productivity.

Educational Chaplaincy: A campus chaplain supports a student struggling with academic pressures and personal issues. The chaplain provides spiritual care through meditation sessions, emotional support through individual counseling, and ethical guidance in making academic and personal decisions. The holistic approach helps the student achieve academic success and personal growth.

Challenges and Opportunities in Holistic Care

Complexity of Needs: One of the challenges in providing holistic care is addressing the complexity of individuals' needs. Chaplains must balance multiple dimensions of care, ensuring that spiritual, emotional, and ethical needs are comprehensively addressed.

Interdisciplinary Coordination: Effective holistic care requires coordination and collaboration with other professionals. Chaplains must navigate interdisciplinary dynamics, communicate effectively, and advocate for the integration of spiritual and ethical care into overall care plans.

Training and Professional Development: Continuous training and professional development are essential for chaplains to provide holistic care. Programs in holistic assessment, interdisciplinary collaboration, and cultural competence equip chaplains with the skills needed to address comprehensive needs.

Innovations in Holistic Care: Innovations in holistic care, such as integrative health practices and technology-enhanced care, offer new opportunities for providing comprehensive support. These advancements enable chaplains to offer holistic care in diverse and evolving contexts, expanding their impact.

The holistic approach is a core principle of chaplaincy, emphasizing the integration of spiritual, emotional, and ethical care into a cohesive practice. By addressing the comprehensive needs of individuals, chaplains foster overall well-being and harmony. The dimensions of holistic care—holistic assessment, integrated care plans, cultural competence, and ongoing evaluation—highlight the multifaceted nature of this approach.

CHAPTER 03

THEOLOGICAL FOUNDATIONS OF CHAPLAINCY

Biblical and Religious Texts: Examining the Theological Underpinnings of Chaplaincy in Various Religious Traditions

Theological foundations are crucial to understanding the role and function of chaplaincy across different religious traditions. This chapter explores the biblical and religious texts that inform and guide chaplaincy practices. By examining these texts, we aim to understand the theological principles that underpin chaplaincy and how they shape the care provided by chaplains.

The Judeo-Christian Tradition

Old Testament Foundations:

1. Priestly Role: The Old Testament presents numerous examples of spiritual leadership and pastoral care. The Levitical priests, for example, were responsible for conducting sacrifices, maintaining temple rituals, and offering pastoral care to the Israelites. Passages such as Leviticus 16:29-34 describe the Day of Atonement, where priests played a crucial role in the spiritual cleansing of the community.

2. Prophetic Ministry: Prophets such as Isaiah, Jeremiah, and Ezekiel provided spiritual guidance, moral counsel, and comfort to the people of Israel. Isaiah 61:1-2, which speaks of the Spirit of the Lord anointing the prophet to bring good news to the afflicted and bind up the brokenhearted, encapsulates the essence of chaplaincy.

New Testament Foundations:

1. Jesus as the Good Shepherd: Jesus Christ serves as the ultimate model for chaplaincy. John 10:11-14 describes Jesus as the Good Shepherd who knows his sheep and lays down his life for them. His ministry of healing, teaching, and comforting provides a blueprint for chaplains.

2. The Great Commission: In Matthew 28:19-20, Jesus commissions his disciples to go and make disciples of all

nations, baptizing them and teaching them to obey all that he commanded. This passage highlights the evangelistic and teaching aspects of chaplaincy.

3. Pastoral Epistles: The letters to Timothy and Titus provide guidance for pastoral care and leadership. 1 Timothy 4:12-16 and Titus 1:7-9 emphasize qualities such as teaching, moral integrity, and spiritual oversight, which are essential for chaplaincy.

The Islamic Tradition

The Quran:

1. Compassion and Mercy: The Quran emphasizes compassion and mercy as central tenets of Islamic faith. Surah Al-Baqarah (2:177) outlines the virtues of righteousness, including faith, charity, and patience. These principles guide the pastoral care provided by Muslim chaplains.

2. Community Care: Surah Al-Ma'idah (5:32) underscores the sanctity of human life and the importance of saving lives. This verse informs the chaplain's role in providing spiritual and emotional support to those in need.

The Hadith:

1. Prophet Muhammad's Example: The Hadith, which records the sayings and actions of Prophet Muhammad, provides numerous examples of pastoral care. For instance, Prophet Muhammad's emphasis on visiting the sick,

comforting the grieving, and supporting the needy reflects the core functions of chaplaincy.

2. Moral Guidance: Hadith collections such as Sahih Bukhari and Sahih Muslim contain teachings on ethical behavior, compassion, and community support, which are integral to the practice of chaplaincy.

The Buddhist Tradition

The Pali Canon:

1. The Four Noble Truths and Eightfold Path: Central to Buddhist teachings, these principles provide a framework for addressing suffering and promoting well-being. The chaplain's role in alleviating suffering and guiding individuals on a path to spiritual and emotional health is rooted in these teachings.

2. Compassion (Karuna) and Loving-Kindness (Metta): The Pali Canon emphasizes the importance of compassion and loving-kindness in relationships. Chaplains embody these qualities in their care for others, fostering an environment of empathy and support.

The Dhammapada:

1. Ethical Living: Verses from the Dhammapada, such as Dhammapada 183, which advocates for avoiding evil, doing good, and purifying the mind, inform the ethical

guidance provided by chaplains. These teachings encourage moral integrity and spiritual growth.

The Hindu Tradition

The Vedas and Upanishads:

1. Dharma: The concept of dharma, or righteous duty, is central to Hindu teachings. The Bhagavad Gita, part of the Mahabharata, elaborates on dharma, particularly in the context of moral and ethical decision-making. Chaplains draw on these texts to provide ethical guidance and support.

2. Compassion and Service: The Upanishads and other Hindu scriptures emphasize compassion and selfless service (seva). Chaplains incorporate these principles into their practice, offering care that is grounded in compassion and a commitment to serving others.

The Bhagavad Gita:

1. Spiritual Guidance: In the Bhagavad Gita, Lord Krishna provides Arjuna with spiritual and ethical guidance in times of crisis. This narrative highlights the role of the chaplain in offering counsel and support during challenging times.

The Jewish Tradition

The Torah:

1. Pastoral Care: The Torah contains numerous examples of pastoral care and spiritual leadership. The role of Moses as a shepherd and leader, guiding the Israelites through

the wilderness, exemplifies the chaplain's role in providing spiritual and emotional support.

2. Ethical Teachings: The ethical teachings of the Torah, such as those found in Leviticus 19:18 ("Love your neighbor as yourself"), underpin the moral guidance provided by chaplains. These teachings emphasize compassion, justice, and community care.

The Talmud:

1. Rabbinic Guidance: The Talmud, a central text in Rabbinic Judaism, provides extensive discussions on ethics, law, and pastoral care. Chaplains draw on these teachings to offer ethical counsel and support to individuals and communities.

2. Healing and Comfort: Rabbinic teachings emphasize the importance of visiting the sick (bikkur cholim) and providing comfort to the bereaved. These practices are integral to the chaplain's role in offering holistic care.

The Sikh Tradition

The Guru Granth Sahib:

1. Compassion and Service: Central to Sikh teachings is the principle of selfless service (seva) and compassion (daya). The Guru Granth Sahib, the holy scripture of Sikhism, emphasizes these values, guiding chaplains in their care for others.

2. Spiritual Support: The teachings of the Sikh Gurus, as recorded in the Guru Granth Sahib, provide spiritual support and guidance. Chaplains draw on these teachings to offer counsel and comfort, helping individuals navigate life's challenges.

The Rehat Maryada:

1. Code of Conduct: The Rehat Maryada, the Sikh code of conduct, outlines ethical and moral principles that guide the practice of chaplaincy. These principles emphasize integrity, humility, and respect, which are essential qualities for chaplains.

The Interfaith Perspective

Common Ethical Principles:

1. Respect and Dignity: Across religious traditions, the principles of respect and dignity are paramount. Chaplains uphold these principles, ensuring that all individuals are treated with honor and compassion.

2. Compassion and Empathy: The universal values of compassion and empathy underpin the care provided by chaplains. These values guide chaplains in offering support that is both heartfelt and meaningful.

3. Justice and Integrity: Ethical guidance across religious traditions emphasizes justice and integrity. Chaplains promote these values, helping individuals make decisions that reflect fairness and moral clarity.

Interfaith Dialogue and Cooperation:

1. Building Bridges: In a multicultural and pluralistic society, chaplains often engage in interfaith dialogue and cooperation. This engagement fosters mutual understanding, respect, and collaboration, enriching the practice of chaplaincy.

2. Inclusive Care: Chaplains provide inclusive care that respects and honors diverse religious and spiritual backgrounds. This approach ensures that all individuals receive meaningful support, regardless of their faith tradition.

The theological foundations of chaplaincy are deeply rooted in biblical and religious texts across various traditions. These texts provide the ethical principles, spiritual guidance, and pastoral practices that inform and shape chaplaincy. By drawing on these rich theological resources, chaplains offer holistic care that addresses the spiritual, emotional, and ethical needs of individuals.

Interfaith Dynamics: The Importance of Interfaith Understanding and Respect in Chaplaincy

In today's diverse and multicultural world, chaplains often serve in environments where they encounter individuals from various religious and spiritual backgrounds. Interfaith understanding and respect are crucial components of effective chaplaincy, enabling chaplains to provide meaningful and inclusive care. This chapter explores the significance of interfaith dynamics in chaplaincy, examining the principles and practices that foster mutual understanding, respect, and cooperation.

Understanding Interfaith Dynamics

Defining Interfaith Dynamics: Interfaith dynamics refer to the interactions and relationships between individuals and groups from different religious and spiritual traditions. These dynamics encompass understanding, respecting, and valuing diverse beliefs, practices, and worldviews.

The Importance of Interfaith Understanding and Respect: Interfaith understanding and respect are essential for promoting harmony, reducing conflict, and fostering a sense of community in diverse settings. In chaplaincy, these principles enable chaplains to provide inclusive care that honors the unique spiritual needs of each individual.

The Role of Chaplains in Promoting Interfaith Understanding

Building Relationships Across Faith Traditions: Chaplains play a crucial role in building relationships across faith traditions. By engaging with individuals from different religious backgrounds, chaplains foster mutual understanding and create a supportive environment for interfaith dialogue and cooperation.

Education and Awareness: Chaplains promote interfaith understanding by educating themselves and others about different religious traditions. This education includes learning about beliefs, practices, rituals, and cultural contexts, enabling chaplains to provide informed and respectful care.

Facilitating Interfaith Dialogue: Chaplains often facilitate interfaith dialogue, creating spaces where individuals can share their beliefs and experiences. These dialogues promote mutual respect, reduce misconceptions, and build bridges between different faith communities.

Providing Inclusive Spiritual Care: Inclusive spiritual care involves recognizing and respecting the diverse religious needs of individuals. Chaplains offer support that is sensitive to different beliefs and practices, ensuring that all individuals receive meaningful and respectful care.

Principles of Interfaith Engagement

Respect for Diversity: Respect for diversity is foundational to interfaith engagement. Chaplains honor the unique beliefs and practices of each individual, recognizing the inherent value and dignity of all faith traditions.

Mutual Learning and Growth: Interfaith engagement is an opportunity for mutual learning and growth. Chaplains approach interfaith interactions with humility and openness, seeking to understand and learn from others' perspectives.

Empathy and Compassion: Empathy and compassion are crucial in interfaith engagement. Chaplains listen with an open heart, seeking to understand the experiences and feelings of individuals from different faith backgrounds.

Shared Ethical Values: Despite differences in beliefs and practices, many religious traditions share common ethical values, such as compassion, justice, and respect for human dignity. Chaplains highlight these shared values, fostering a sense of common ground and mutual respect.

The Impact of Interfaith Understanding and Respect

Enhanced Quality of Care: Interfaith understanding and respect enhance the quality of care provided by chaplains. By recognizing and honoring diverse spiritual needs, chaplains offer support that is meaningful, relevant, and respectful.

Strengthened Community Cohesion: Interfaith engagement fosters community cohesion by promoting mutual understanding and reducing conflict. Chaplains help build inclusive communities where individuals from different faith traditions feel valued and respected.

Personal and Spiritual Growth: Interfaith interactions contribute to personal and spiritual growth for both chaplains and those they serve. Exposure to different perspectives enriches spiritual understanding and fosters a deeper appreciation for the diversity of human experience.

Promotion of Peace and Harmony: By fostering interfaith understanding and respect, chaplains contribute to the promotion of peace and harmony. Their work helps create environments where individuals can coexist peacefully and work together for the common good.

Case Studies in Interfaith Chaplaincy

Healthcare Chaplaincy: In a hospital setting, a chaplain provides interfaith support to patients from various religious backgrounds. The chaplain collaborates with local faith leaders to ensure that patients receive appropriate spiritual care, respecting their unique beliefs and practices.

Military Chaplaincy: A military chaplain serves a diverse group of service members, facilitating interfaith worship services and discussion groups. The chaplain creates an inclusive environment where individuals can share their faith experiences and find mutual support.

Corporate Chaplaincy: In a corporate environment, a chaplain supports employees from different religious traditions by organizing interfaith events and educational workshops. The chaplain promotes a culture of respect and understanding, enhancing workplace harmony and collaboration.

Educational Chaplaincy: A campus chaplain facilitates interfaith dialogue among students, creating opportunities for learning and mutual respect. The chaplain organizes interfaith panels, discussion groups, and cultural events, fostering an inclusive campus community.

Challenges and Opportunities in Interfaith Chaplaincy

Navigating Religious Differences: One of the challenges in interfaith chaplaincy is navigating religious differences and potential conflicts. Chaplains must approach these challenges with sensitivity, seeking common ground and promoting mutual respect.

Overcoming Prejudice and Misunderstanding: Prejudice and misunderstanding can hinder interfaith engagement. Chaplains play a crucial role in addressing these issues by promoting education, empathy, and open dialogue.

Balancing Inclusivity and Specificity: Chaplains must balance the need for inclusive care with the specific spiritual needs of individuals. This balance requires a deep understanding of different faith traditions and the ability to provide personalized support.

Leveraging Interfaith Opportunities: Interfaith chaplaincy presents numerous opportunities for learning, growth, and collaboration. Chaplains can leverage these opportunities to foster mutual understanding, build inclusive communities, and promote social harmony.

Interfaith understanding and respect are vital components of effective chaplaincy. By promoting these principles, chaplains provide inclusive and meaningful care that honors the diverse spiritual needs of individuals. The role of chaplains in building relationships, facilitating dialogue, and providing education underscores the importance of interfaith engagement in fostering harmony and mutual respect.

The Role of Prayer and Ritual: How Prayer, Sacraments, and Rituals Play a Vital Role in Chaplaincy Work

Prayer and ritual are fundamental aspects of chaplaincy, serving as vital tools for providing spiritual support, fostering community, and facilitating personal transformation. This chapter explores the significance of prayer, sacraments, and rituals in chaplaincy work, examining how these practices enhance the holistic care provided by chaplains across various settings.

Understanding Prayer and Ritual

Defining Prayer and Ritual: Prayer is a spiritual practice that involves communication with the divine, expressing praise, gratitude, confession, and supplication. Rituals are structured, symbolic actions performed in a prescribed manner, often marking significant life events or religious observances.

The Importance of Prayer and Ritual: Prayer and ritual play crucial roles in spiritual well-being, offering comfort, meaning, and connection. These practices help individuals navigate life's challenges, celebrate important milestones, and deepen their spiritual lives.

The Role of Prayer in Chaplaincy

Personal and Communal Prayer: Chaplains facilitate both personal and communal prayer, providing opportunities for individuals to connect with the divine. Personal prayer allows individuals to express their deepest thoughts and feelings, while communal prayer fosters a sense of unity and shared spiritual experience.

Intercessory Prayer: Intercessory prayer involves praying on behalf of others, offering support and compassion in times of need. Chaplains often lead intercessory prayers for individuals facing illness, loss, or other challenges, providing spiritual comfort and hope.

Guided Meditation and Contemplation: Chaplains use guided meditation and contemplative practices to help individuals achieve a state of spiritual and emotional calm. These practices can include mindfulness, breathwork, and visualization, enhancing overall well-being.

Healing and Comfort: Prayer serves as a powerful source of healing and comfort. Chaplains use prayer to support individuals experiencing physical, emotional, or spiritual pain, offering solace and strength.

The Role of Ritual in Chaplaincy

Sacraments and Rites of Passage: Sacraments and rites of passage mark significant moments in an individual's spiritual journey. Chaplains administer sacraments such as baptism, communion, and anointing of the sick, as well as conduct rituals for births, marriages, and funerals.

Daily and Seasonal Rituals: Daily and seasonal rituals provide structure and meaning to the rhythms of life. Chaplains lead rituals for various religious observances, such as daily prayers, weekly services, and annual celebrations, helping individuals connect with their faith traditions.

Symbolic Actions: Rituals often involve symbolic actions that convey deeper spiritual meanings. Chaplains incorporate symbols such as lighting candles, anointing with oil, or sharing bread and wine, enhancing the spiritual experience of individuals and communities.

Community Building: Rituals play a vital role in building and sustaining community. Chaplains use rituals to foster a sense of belonging and shared identity, strengthening communal bonds and supporting collective spiritual growth.

The Impact of Prayer and Ritual

Spiritual Connection: Prayer and ritual facilitate a deep sense of connection with the divine, enhancing spiritual well-being. These practices help individuals cultivate a personal relationship with their faith, providing a source of guidance, inspiration, and strength.

Emotional Healing and Resilience: Prayer and ritual offer emotional healing and resilience by providing a framework for expressing and processing emotions. These practices help individuals navigate grief, loss, and trauma, promoting emotional stability and recovery.

Meaning and Purpose: Rituals imbue life events with meaning and purpose, helping individuals understand and celebrate the significance of these moments. Chaplains use rituals to mark transitions, honor achievements, and provide closure, contributing to a sense of fulfillment and continuity.

Community Cohesion: Communal prayer and ritual foster a sense of unity and belonging, strengthening community cohesion. Chaplains create inclusive and supportive environments where individuals can share their spiritual journeys and support one another.

Case Studies in Prayer and Ritual

Healthcare Chaplaincy: In a hospital, a chaplain uses prayer and ritual to support a patient undergoing surgery. The chaplain offers a pre-surgery prayer for strength and healing, conducts a bedside communion, and leads a thanksgiving prayer after the successful procedure, providing comfort and spiritual support throughout the process.

Military Chaplaincy: A military chaplain leads rituals and prayers for soldiers before deployment. The chaplain conducts a blessing ceremony, offers intercessory prayers for protection, and provides individual prayer sessions, fostering a sense of spiritual readiness and community solidarity.

Corporate Chaplaincy: In a corporate setting, a chaplain uses prayer and ritual to support employees during a period of organizational change. The chaplain leads a mindfulness meditation session to reduce stress, offers a prayer for guidance and resilience, and conducts a ritual to mark the transition, helping employees navigate the changes with a sense of purpose and support.

Educational Chaplaincy: A campus chaplain leads prayer and ritual activities for students during finals week. The chaplain offers a prayer for focus and calm, conducts a communal candle-lighting ceremony to symbolize hope and perseverance, and provides guided meditation sessions, supporting students' spiritual and emotional well-being.

Challenges and Opportunities in Integrating Prayer and Ritual

Diverse Beliefs and Practices: One of the challenges in integrating prayer and ritual is accommodating diverse beliefs and practices. Chaplains must be sensitive to different religious traditions and create inclusive environments that respect and honor these differences.

Balancing Tradition and Innovation: Chaplains must balance traditional religious practices with innovative approaches that resonate with contemporary individuals. This balance requires creativity and flexibility, ensuring that prayer and ritual remain relevant and meaningful.

Training and Professional Development: Continuous training and professional development are essential for chaplains to effectively integrate prayer and ritual into their practice. Programs in liturgical studies, pastoral care, and interfaith engagement equip chaplains with the skills needed to provide inclusive and impactful spiritual support.

Expanding the Reach of Prayer and Ritual: Innovations in technology and communication offer new opportunities for expanding the reach of prayer and ritual. Chaplains can use virtual platforms to conduct prayer sessions, lead rituals, and provide spiritual support to individuals and communities in diverse and remote settings.

Prayer and ritual are integral to the practice of chaplaincy, providing essential tools for spiritual support, emotional healing, and community building. By integrating these practices into their work, chaplains enhance the holistic care they provide, addressing the spiritual, emotional, and ethical needs of individuals.

CHAPTER 04

MILITARY CHAPLAINCY

Historical Role: The Evolution of Military Chaplaincy from Ancient Times to the Present

Military chaplaincy has a long and storied history, evolving significantly from its ancient origins to the structured and professional roles we recognize today. This chapter explores the development of military chaplaincy, examining how chaplains have provided spiritual, emotional, and ethical support to soldiers across different eras and conflicts.

Ancient Military Chaplaincy

Early Spiritual Leaders: The concept of military chaplaincy can be traced back to ancient civilizations, where spiritual leaders accompanied warriors into battle. In ancient

Egypt, priests offered prayers and rituals to ensure divine favor for the army. Similarly, in ancient Greece and Rome, religious figures known as augurs and pontiffs performed rituals to seek the gods' blessings before battles.

Hebrew Tradition: The Hebrew Bible provides examples of spiritual leaders who served military functions. Priests and prophets, such as Samuel, who anointed Saul and David as kings, played vital roles in guiding and supporting the Israelites in their military endeavors. The Ark of the Covenant, carried by priests, often accompanied the Israelite army, symbolizing God's presence and favor.

Medieval Military Chaplaincy

The Crusades: The Crusades (11th to 13th centuries) marked a significant period for military chaplaincy. Chaplains accompanied Christian crusaders on their campaigns to the Holy Land, providing spiritual care, conducting religious services, and offering moral support. Orders such as the Knights Templar and the Knights Hospitaller included chaplains who played crucial roles in maintaining the spiritual well-being of the knights.

Royal Chaplains: In medieval Europe, chaplains served in the courts of kings and nobles, accompanying them on military campaigns. These royal chaplains provided religious services, spiritual counsel, and moral guidance to the rulers and their armies. The presence of chaplains underscored the close relationship between the church and the state during this period.

The Role of Monasteries: Monasteries also played a role in supporting military chaplaincy. Monastic orders, such as the Benedictines, offered prayers for soldiers and provided sanctuary and care for the wounded and sick. Monks and priests from these orders sometimes accompanied armies, offering spiritual support on the battlefield.

Early Modern Military Chaplaincy

The Reformation and Religious Wars: The Reformation (16th century) and the ensuing religious wars in Europe led to changes in military chaplaincy. Protestant and Catholic chaplains served their respective armies, providing spiritual care and moral support. The Thirty Years' War (1618-1648), a significant religious conflict, saw chaplains playing crucial roles on both sides, highlighting the continued importance of spiritual care in military contexts.

Colonial Armies: As European powers expanded their empires, military chaplains accompanied colonial armies, providing spiritual support to soldiers stationed in distant territories. These chaplains faced unique challenges, including ministering to diverse and often hostile environments and navigating the complexities of colonial rule.

The 18th and 19th Centuries

The American Revolution: During the American Revolution (1775-1783), chaplains served in both the Continental Army and British forces. They provided religious services, moral support, and pastoral care to soldiers. The Continental Congress recognized the importance of chaplaincy, appointing chaplains to regiments and establishing the tradition of military chaplaincy in the United States.

Napoleonic Wars: The Napoleonic Wars (1803-1815) saw the formalization of military chaplaincy in European armies. The British Army, for example, established the Army Chaplains' Department in 1796, highlighting the institutionalization of chaplaincy roles. Chaplains provided spiritual care, conducted religious services, and offered moral support to soldiers during this period of intense and prolonged conflict.

The American Civil War: The American Civil War (1861-1865) further solidified the role of chaplains in the military. Both Union and Confederate armies appointed chaplains to provide spiritual care, moral guidance, and support to soldiers. Chaplains played crucial roles in maintaining morale, addressing the spiritual needs of soldiers, and offering comfort to the wounded and dying.

The 20th Century and World Wars

World War I: World War I (1914-1918) marked a significant evolution in military chaplaincy. The scale and intensity of the conflict highlighted the need for comprehensive spiritual and emotional support for soldiers. Chaplains from various faith traditions served on the front lines, in field hospitals, and in support roles, providing religious services, counseling, and moral support. The experiences of chaplains during World War I led to increased recognition of their contributions and the formalization of their roles within armed forces.

World War II: World War II (1939-1945) saw the further institutionalization and professionalization of military chaplaincy. Chaplains served in every theater of the war, offering spiritual care, conducting religious services, and providing moral guidance. The role of chaplains expanded to include support for prisoners of war, displaced persons, and civilians affected by the conflict. The establishment of chaplaincy training programs and the integration of chaplains into military command structures underscored the importance of their work.

Post-War Period: In the post-war period, military chaplaincy continued to evolve. The Korean War (1950-1953) and the Vietnam War (1955-1975) highlighted the ongoing need for spiritual and emotional support for soldiers. Chaplains played crucial roles in addressing the unique challenges faced by soldiers in these conflicts, including the psychological impact of warfare and the moral complexities of combat.

Contemporary Military Chaplaincy

Modern Conflicts: In contemporary conflicts, such as those in Iraq and Afghanistan, military chaplains continue to provide vital support to soldiers. They address the spiritual and emotional needs of service members, offer ethical guidance, and support the families of deployed soldiers. The role of chaplains has expanded to include support for mental health issues, such as post-traumatic stress disorder (PTSD) and moral injury.

Diversity and Inclusivity: Modern military chaplaincy reflects the increasing diversity and inclusivity of armed forces. Chaplains from various faith traditions, including Christianity, Islam, Judaism, Buddhism, and others, serve alongside each other, providing support to soldiers of all religious backgrounds. This diversity underscores the importance of interfaith understanding and respect in contemporary military chaplaincy.

Training and Professional Development: The professionalization of military chaplaincy includes extensive training and professional development programs. Chaplains receive training in pastoral care, counseling, ethical decision-making, and intercultural competence. This training equips chaplains to address the complex and varied needs of modern soldiers.

Technological Advancements: Technological advancements have also impacted military chaplaincy. Chaplains use digital communication tools to provide remote support to deployed soldiers, offer virtual religious services, and create online communities for spiritual and emotional support. These innovations enhance the reach and effectiveness of military chaplaincy in the digital age.

Key Figures in Military Chaplaincy

Saint Martin of Tours: Regarded as one of the earliest military chaplains, Saint Martin of Tours was a Roman soldier who converted to Christianity and later became a bishop. His life and work symbolize the integration of military and spiritual life.

Chaplain Emil Kapaun: A U.S. Army chaplain during the Korean War, Father Emil Kapaun is remembered for his heroic service, providing spiritual and emotional support to soldiers and fellow prisoners of war. He posthumously received the Medal of Honor for his bravery and sacrifice.

Rabbi Roland Gittelsohn: The first Jewish chaplain to serve in the U.S. Marine Corps, Rabbi Gittelsohn is known for his moving eulogy at the dedication of the Iwo Jima cemetery during World War II. His words emphasized the shared sacrifice and unity of soldiers of all faiths.

Imam Yahya Hendi: As the first Muslim chaplain at Georgetown University and a prominent military chaplain, Imam Hendi has worked to promote interfaith understanding and provide spiritual support to Muslim soldiers in the U.S. military.

The historical role of military chaplaincy reflects the enduring importance of spiritual, emotional, and ethical support for soldiers. From ancient times to the present, chaplains have played crucial roles in maintaining morale, providing comfort, and fostering resilience among military personnel. The evolution of military chaplaincy highlights the adaptability and significance of this vocation in addressing the diverse and complex needs of soldiers across different eras and conflicts.

Spiritual Resilience: How Chaplains Support Soldiers' Spiritual Resilience in Times of War and Peace

Spiritual resilience is a crucial aspect of well-being for soldiers, enabling them to endure the stresses and challenges of military life. Chaplains play a vital role in fostering this resilience, providing support that helps soldiers maintain their spiritual, emotional, and moral strength in both wartime and peacetime. This chapter explores the concept of spiritual resilience, the methods chaplains use to cultivate it, and the impact of their work on the overall well-being of soldiers.

Understanding Spiritual Resilience

Defining Spiritual Resilience: Spiritual resilience refers to the ability to sustain and recover one's sense of purpose, faith, and inner peace in the face of adversity. It involves maintaining a strong spiritual foundation, finding meaning in challenging experiences, and staying connected to one's values and beliefs.

The Importance of Spiritual Resilience: For soldiers, spiritual resilience is essential for coping with the physical, emotional, and moral demands of military service. It provides a source of strength, hope, and guidance, helping soldiers navigate the complexities of combat and the pressures of military life.

The Role of Chaplains in Fostering Spiritual Resilience

Providing Spiritual Guidance: Chaplains offer spiritual guidance to help soldiers connect with their faith and values. This guidance includes facilitating religious practices, providing spiritual counseling, and helping soldiers explore and strengthen their beliefs.

Offering Emotional Support: Chaplains provide emotional support to soldiers, helping them manage stress, grief, and trauma. Through compassionate listening, counseling, and prayer, chaplains create a safe space for soldiers to express their emotions and find solace.

Conducting Religious Services and Rituals: Regular participation in religious services and rituals helps soldiers maintain their spiritual practices and stay connected to their faith communities. Chaplains conduct these services, offering opportunities for worship, reflection, and communal support.

Facilitating Community and Fellowship: Chaplains foster a sense of community and fellowship among soldiers, creating environments where they can share their experiences and support one another. Group activities, such as Bible studies, prayer groups, and discussion circles, build camaraderie and mutual support.

Ethical and Moral Support: Chaplains provide ethical and moral support, helping soldiers navigate the moral complexities of military service. They offer guidance on ethical decision-making, address moral injuries, and support soldiers in aligning their actions with their values.

Methods for Building Spiritual Resilience

Personal Reflection and Meditation: Encouraging soldiers to engage in personal reflection and meditation helps them connect with their inner selves and find peace.

Chaplains guide soldiers in practices such as mindfulness, deep breathing, and contemplative prayer.

Storytelling and Sharing Experiences: Sharing personal stories and experiences allows soldiers to process their emotions and find meaning in their challenges. Chaplains facilitate storytelling sessions where soldiers can express their journeys, fostering a sense of understanding and empathy.

Spiritual Education and Growth: Providing opportunities for spiritual education and growth helps soldiers deepen their knowledge and understanding of their faith. Chaplains offer religious education classes, workshops, and seminars on topics such as theology, ethics, and spiritual practices.

Resilience Training Programs: Chaplains develop and lead resilience training programs that integrate spiritual, emotional, and physical components. These programs teach soldiers practical skills for coping with stress, enhancing their overall resilience.

Access to Resources: Chaplains ensure that soldiers have access to spiritual resources such as religious texts, prayer books, and inspirational literature. These resources support soldiers in their personal spiritual practices and provide comfort in times of need.

The Impact of Spiritual Resilience on Soldiers

Enhanced Coping Mechanisms: Spiritual resilience provides soldiers with effective coping mechanisms for managing stress, trauma, and adversity. Soldiers with strong spiritual resilience are better equipped to handle the psychological and emotional challenges of military life.

Improved Mental Health: Spiritual resilience contributes to improved mental health outcomes, reducing symptoms of anxiety, depression, and post-traumatic stress disorder (PTSD). Soldiers with a strong sense of spiritual well-being experience greater emotional stability and overall mental health.

Increased Sense of Purpose and Meaning: Spiritual resilience helps soldiers find purpose and meaning in their experiences, even in difficult and challenging situations. This sense of purpose motivates soldiers, enhances their commitment to their duties, and fosters a positive outlook on life.

Stronger Ethical and Moral Foundations: Spiritual resilience reinforces soldiers' ethical and moral foundations, guiding their actions and decisions. Soldiers with strong spiritual resilience are more likely to act with integrity, uphold their values, and navigate moral dilemmas effectively.

Greater Sense of Community and Belonging: Spiritual resilience fosters a sense of community and belonging among soldiers, reducing feelings of isolation and loneliness. Soldiers who feel connected to their faith communities and fellow service members experience greater support and camaraderie.

Case Studies in Spiritual Resilience

Deployment Support: During a deployment, a chaplain provides regular spiritual and emotional support to soldiers in a combat zone. The chaplain conducts worship services, leads meditation sessions, and offers individual counseling. These activities help soldiers maintain their spiritual resilience and cope with the stresses of deployment.

Post-Deployment Reintegration: A chaplain supports soldiers returning from deployment by facilitating reintegration programs that include spiritual and emotional components. The chaplain leads group discussions, offers spiritual education classes, and provides resources for personal reflection. These efforts help soldiers transition back to civilian life and strengthen their spiritual resilience.

Support During Training: In a military training environment, a chaplain offers resilience training programs that integrate spiritual practices. The chaplain conducts workshops on mindfulness, ethical decision-making, and stress management. These programs enhance soldiers' resilience and prepare them for the challenges of military service.

Crisis Intervention: A chaplain supports a soldier experiencing a personal crisis by providing immediate spiritual and emotional care. The chaplain offers a listening ear, leads the soldier in prayer, and provides guidance on navigating the crisis. This support helps the soldier find strength and resilience in the face of adversity.

Challenges and Opportunities in Fostering Spiritual Resilience

Diverse Beliefs and Practices: One of the challenges in fostering spiritual resilience is accommodating the diverse beliefs and practices of soldiers. Chaplains must be sensitive to different religious traditions and provide inclusive support that respects and honors these differences.

Balancing Operational Demands: Chaplains must balance the demands of military operations with the need to provide spiritual care. This balance requires flexibility and creativity, ensuring that spiritual support is integrated into the daily routines and activities of soldiers.

Addressing Moral Injury: Moral injury, which occurs when soldiers' actions or experiences violate their moral beliefs, presents a significant challenge to spiritual resilience. Chaplains play a crucial role in addressing moral injury by providing ethical guidance, facilitating healing rituals, and offering compassionate support.

Leveraging Technological Advancements: Technological advancements offer new opportunities for fostering spiritual resilience. Chaplains can use digital communication tools to provide remote support, create online communities, and offer virtual religious services, expanding their reach and impact.

Spiritual resilience is essential for soldiers, providing the strength and stability needed to endure the challenges of military life. Chaplains play a vital role in fostering this resilience, offering spiritual guidance, emotional support, and ethical counsel. Through personal reflection, communal activities, resilience training, and access to resources, chaplains help soldiers build and maintain their spiritual resilience in times of war and peace.

Ethical Dilemmas: Navigating the Ethical Challenges Faced by Military Chaplains

Military chaplains operate in environments where ethical dilemmas are a constant reality. The unique context of military service, with its inherent challenges and complexities, often places chaplains in situations that require careful ethical consideration and decision-making. This chapter explores the ethical dilemmas faced by military chaplains, the principles guiding their responses, and the impact of their decisions on soldiers and the broader military community.

Understanding Ethical Dilemmas in Military Chaplaincy

Defining Ethical Dilemmas: Ethical dilemmas occur when chaplains are faced with situations where there are conflicting moral principles or values, making it difficult to determine the right course of action. These dilemmas often involve complex considerations of duty, loyalty, justice, and compassion.

The Importance of Ethical Decision-Making: Effective ethical decision-making is crucial for maintaining moral integrity, trust, and credibility. Chaplains must navigate these dilemmas thoughtfully to provide appropriate guidance and support to soldiers while upholding their own ethical standards.

Common Ethical Dilemmas Faced by Military Chaplains

Confidentiality vs. Duty to Report: One of the most challenging ethical dilemmas for military chaplains is balancing confidentiality with the duty to report certain information. For instance, when a soldier confides in a chaplain about suicidal thoughts, substance abuse, or illegal activities, the chaplain must weigh the importance of confidentiality against the need to protect the individual and others from harm.

Dual Loyalty: Chaplains often face the dilemma of dual loyalty, where they must balance their commitment to the military mission with their pastoral responsibility to support soldiers' well-being. This can be particularly challenging when the needs of individual soldiers conflict with military objectives or policies.

Moral Injury and Combat Ethics: Chaplains frequently encounter soldiers struggling with moral injury—emotional and spiritual distress resulting from actions in combat that violate their moral or ethical beliefs. Providing support to these soldiers while addressing the broader ethical implications of warfare presents a significant challenge.

Religious Accommodation vs. Military Requirements: Chaplains must navigate the tension between accommodating soldiers' religious practices and adhering to military requirements. This can include issues such as providing time and space for religious observances, dietary restrictions, and dress code accommodations.

Non-Judgmental Support vs. Ethical Standards: Chaplains are called to provide non-judgmental support to all soldiers, regardless of their actions or beliefs. However, they must also uphold ethical standards and sometimes confront behaviors or attitudes that are morally or legally problematic.

Principles Guiding Ethical Decision-Making

Respect for Autonomy: Chaplains must respect the autonomy of soldiers, supporting their right to make informed decisions about their own lives. This principle involves providing soldiers with the information and guidance they need while honoring their personal choices.

Beneficence and Non-Maleficence: The principles of beneficence (doing good) and non-maleficence (avoiding harm) guide chaplains in their efforts to promote the well-being of soldiers and prevent harm. These principles help chaplains navigate dilemmas where the potential benefits and harms of different actions must be weighed.

Justice and Fairness: Chaplains must ensure that their actions are just and fair, treating all soldiers equitably and without bias. This principle involves advocating for soldiers' rights and ensuring that resources and support are distributed fairly.

Confidentiality and Trust: Maintaining confidentiality is crucial for building trust between chaplains and soldiers. Chaplains must carefully consider when it is ethically permissible or necessary to break confidentiality to protect individuals or the community.

Professional and Ethical Integrity: Chaplains must uphold professional and ethical standards, ensuring that their actions align with their moral values and the ethical codes of their profession. This principle involves continuous self-reflection and accountability.

Strategies for Navigating Ethical Dilemmas

Ethical Decision-Making Models: Chaplains can use structured ethical decision-making models to navigate complex dilemmas. These models provide a systematic approach to evaluating the ethical dimensions of a situation, considering possible courses of action, and making informed decisions.

Consultation and Collaboration: Seeking guidance from colleagues, supervisors, and ethics committees can help chaplains navigate ethical dilemmas. Collaborative discussions provide diverse perspectives and shared wisdom, supporting more balanced and informed decision-making.

Ongoing Education and Training: Continuous education and training in ethics help chaplains stay informed about ethical principles, emerging issues, and best practices. Professional development opportunities, such as workshops, seminars, and courses, enhance chaplains' ethical competence.

Reflective Practice: Engaging in reflective practice allows chaplains to critically examine their experiences, decisions, and actions. Reflective journals, peer discussions, and supervision sessions support chaplains in learning from their experiences and improving their ethical decision-making skills.

Support Networks: Building and maintaining support networks with other chaplains, mental health professionals, and trusted advisors provide a source of support and guidance. These networks offer a safe space for discussing ethical challenges and seeking advice.

Case Studies in Ethical Dilemmas

Confidentiality vs. Duty to Report: A chaplain is approached by a soldier who confides that he is struggling with severe depression and has had thoughts of self-harm. The chaplain must decide whether to maintain confidentiality or report the soldier's condition to ensure he receives the necessary mental health support. The chaplain consults with mental health professionals and uses an ethical decision-making model to determine that reporting the soldier's condition is necessary to protect his well-being while ensuring that the soldier is supported through the process.

Dual Loyalty: During a combat deployment, a chaplain is asked to support a mission that involves actions the chaplain finds morally troubling. The chaplain must balance their loyalty to the military mission with their responsibility to support the spiritual and moral well-being of the soldiers. The chaplain seeks guidance from senior chaplains and reflects on the ethical implications of the mission, ultimately deciding to provide support while also advocating for the ethical considerations of the soldiers involved.

Moral Injury: A soldier confides in a chaplain about experiencing moral injury after participating in a combat operation that resulted in civilian casualties. The chaplain provides non-judgmental support and helps the soldier process his emotions while also addressing the broader ethical implications of the operation. The chaplain collaborates with mental health professionals to provide comprehensive care and facilitates discussions on ethical decision-making in combat.

Religious Accommodation: A Muslim soldier requests time off for daily prayers, which conflicts with the unit's training schedule. The chaplain must navigate the tension between accommodating the soldier's religious practice and adhering to the training requirements. The chaplain works with the unit's leadership to find a compromise that allows the soldier to fulfill his religious obligations while participating in essential training activities.

Non-Judgmental Support vs. Ethical Standards: A chaplain encounters a soldier who admits to engaging in unethical behavior, such as hazing a fellow soldier. The chaplain provides non-judgmental support but also addresses the unethical behavior by guiding the soldier in understanding the impact of his actions and encouraging him to take responsibility. The chaplain reports the behavior to the appropriate authorities to ensure that it is addressed within the military's ethical framework.

Navigating ethical dilemmas is a core component of military chaplaincy, requiring careful consideration, compassion, and integrity. By adhering to ethical principles and employing strategies for ethical decision-making, chaplains can effectively address the complex challenges they encounter in their work. The ability to navigate these dilemmas not only supports the well-being of soldiers but also upholds the moral integrity and credibility of the chaplaincy.

Stories from the Field: Anecdotes and Case Studies Highlighting the Impact of Military Chaplains

Military chaplains play a crucial role in the lives of soldiers, providing spiritual, emotional, and ethical support in various challenging situations. This chapter presents a collection of anecdotes and case studies that highlight the profound impact military chaplains have on individuals and units. These stories from the field illustrate the diverse ways chaplains make a difference in the military context.

Supporting Soldiers in Combat Zones

A Chaplain's Prayer in Afghanistan:

During a deployment in Afghanistan, Chaplain Michael served with a battalion frequently engaged in combat operations. One evening, as the unit prepared for a night patrol, the soldiers gathered around Chaplain Michael for a pre-mission prayer. He offered words of protection and courage, invoking a sense of peace and confidence among the troops. Throughout the patrol, the soldiers felt reassured by the chaplain's prayer, which strengthened their resolve and unity. Chaplain Michael's presence and prayers provided spiritual resilience, helping the soldiers face the dangers ahead.

Comforting the Wounded:

In a field hospital in Iraq, Chaplain Sarah encountered a young soldier severely injured by an improvised explosive device (IED). The soldier was in intense pain and emotionally distressed, fearing for his future. Chaplain Sarah sat by his bedside, holding his hand and offering words of comfort and hope. She prayed with him, helping to ease his anxiety and pain. Over the following weeks, Chaplain Sarah visited him regularly, providing spiritual support and counseling. Her compassionate care played a crucial role in the soldier's emotional healing and recovery.

Providing Moral and Ethical Guidance

Navigating Moral Injury:

Sergeant James, a veteran of multiple deployments, struggled with moral injury after participating in a combat operation that resulted in civilian casualties. He felt profound guilt and questioned the morality of his actions. Chaplain David, known for his empathetic listening and non-judgmental approach, provided a safe space for Sergeant James to express his feelings. Through numerous conversations, prayers, and ethical discussions, Chaplain David helped Sergeant James process his emotions and find a path to forgiveness and moral reconciliation. This support was pivotal in helping Sergeant James regain his sense of purpose and moral clarity.

Addressing Ethical Dilemmas:

Lieutenant Emily faced an ethical dilemma when she discovered that her unit was involved in questionable activities that violated military ethics. Torn between her loyalty to her comrades and her commitment to ethical conduct, she sought guidance from Chaplain Mark. He listened attentively, offered moral counsel, and helped her explore the ethical implications of her situation. Together, they devised a plan to address the issue through proper channels while protecting her integrity. Chaplain Mark's guidance empowered Lieutenant Emily to act ethically, demonstrating the crucial role chaplains play in navigating moral complexities.

Fostering Community and Resilience

Building Unit Cohesion:

During a deployment to a remote base, Chaplain Rachel noticed a growing sense of isolation and tension among the soldiers. She organized regular gatherings that included communal meals, prayer services, and group discussions. These activities provided opportunities for soldiers to share their experiences, support one another, and build camaraderie. Chaplain Rachel's efforts fostered a strong sense of community, improving morale and resilience. The unit became more cohesive and better able to cope with the challenges of their deployment.

Resilience Workshops:

In a training environment, Chaplain John conducted resilience workshops for new recruits facing the rigors of basic training. These workshops included mindfulness exercises, stress management techniques, and discussions on spiritual resilience. Chaplain John's approachable manner and practical advice helped the recruits develop coping strategies and build inner strength. His workshops were highly appreciated, and many recruits reported feeling better equipped to handle the physical and emotional demands of military training.

Supporting Families and Loved Ones

Grief Counseling:

When a soldier in her unit was killed in action, Chaplain Maria provided grief counseling to his grieving family. She visited the family, offering prayers, listening to their stories, and providing comfort during their time of loss. Chaplain Maria helped organize the memorial service, ensuring it honored the soldier's life and faith. Her compassionate presence and support were invaluable to the family, helping them navigate their grief and find solace in their faith.

Supporting Military Spouses:

During a long deployment, Chaplain Kevin organized support groups for military spouses left behind. These groups provided a space for spouses to share their concerns, offer mutual support, and receive spiritual guidance. Chaplain Kevin facilitated discussions on coping with separation, maintaining strong relationships, and finding strength in their faith. The support groups became a vital resource for the spouses, fostering a sense of community and resilience during the challenging months of deployment.

Addressing Mental Health Challenges

Crisis Intervention:

Late one night, Chaplain Andrew received an urgent call from a soldier in crisis. The soldier, struggling with severe depression and thoughts of suicide, reached out to Chaplain Andrew as a last resort. Chaplain Andrew immediately responded, meeting the soldier in person. He provided a compassionate and non-judgmental presence, offering words of hope and reassurance. Chaplain Andrew stayed with the soldier, prayed with him, and helped him access mental health services. His timely intervention and ongoing support were crucial in saving the soldier's life and guiding him towards recovery.

Post-Traumatic Stress Disorder (PTSD) Support:

Chaplain Lisa worked closely with soldiers suffering from PTSD after returning from combat deployments. She led support groups where soldiers could share their experiences, learn coping strategies, and find spiritual solace. Chaplain Lisa also provided individual counseling, helping soldiers process their trauma and reconnect with their faith. Her dedicated support made a significant difference in the lives of many soldiers, aiding their journey towards healing and recovery.

Promoting Interfaith Understanding and Respect

Interfaith Services:

In a diverse military unit, Chaplain Thomas organized interfaith services to accommodate the varied religious backgrounds of the soldiers. These services included prayers, readings, and reflections from different faith traditions, promoting mutual respect and understanding. Chaplain Thomas fostered an inclusive environment where all soldiers felt valued and supported in their spiritual practices. His efforts strengthened the unit's cohesion and demonstrated the importance of interfaith respect in the military.

Cultural Sensitivity Training:

Recognizing the importance of cultural competence, Chaplain Jessica conducted cultural sensitivity training for her unit before deploying to a region with different religious and cultural norms. She educated the soldiers on local customs, religious practices, and the importance of respecting cultural differences. Chaplain Jessica's training helped the soldiers build positive relationships with local communities and navigate their deployment with cultural awareness and respect.

These stories from the field illustrate the profound impact military chaplains have on the lives of soldiers and their families. Through spiritual guidance, emotional support, ethical counsel, and community-building efforts, chaplains provide essential care in both wartime and peacetime. Their presence and actions demonstrate the unique and invaluable role of military chaplains in fostering resilience, moral integrity, and holistic well-being within the military community.

Role in Hospitals: The Essential Functions of Chaplains in Hospital Settings

Healthcare chaplaincy is a specialized field that addresses the spiritual, emotional, and ethical needs of patients, families, and healthcare staff. In hospital settings, chaplains play a crucial role in providing holistic care, supporting individuals through some of the most challenging moments of their lives. This chapter explores the essential functions of chaplains in hospitals, highlighting the impact of their work on patient care and the broader healthcare environment.

Understanding Healthcare Chaplaincy

Defining Healthcare Chaplaincy: Healthcare chaplaincy involves providing spiritual and emotional support to patients, their families, and healthcare staff within medical settings. Chaplains offer pastoral care, facilitate religious and spiritual practices, and address ethical concerns, contributing to the overall well-being of those they serve.

The Importance of Chaplaincy in Healthcare: The presence of chaplains in hospitals enhances the quality of care by addressing the holistic needs of patients. Spiritual care is integral to healing and coping, offering comfort, meaning, and hope in the face of illness and uncertainty.

Essential Functions of Hospital Chaplains

Providing Spiritual Care to Patients:

1. Bedside Visits: Chaplains visit patients at their bedsides, offering a compassionate presence and listening to their concerns. These visits provide opportunities for patients to express their fears, hopes, and spiritual needs, receiving support tailored to their individual circumstances.

2. Prayer and Sacraments: Chaplains lead patients in prayer and administer sacraments, such as communion, anointing of the sick, and last rites. These spiritual practices offer comfort, strengthen faith, and provide a sense of peace during critical moments.

3. Spiritual Assessments: Chaplains conduct spiritual assessments to understand patients' spiritual backgrounds, beliefs, and needs. This information guides the provision of personalized spiritual care, ensuring that support aligns with patients' values and preferences.

Supporting Families:

1. Emotional and Spiritual Support: Chaplains provide emotional and spiritual support to families dealing with a loved one's illness or hospitalization. They offer a listening

ear, comfort, and guidance, helping families navigate their fears and uncertainties.

2. Facilitating Communication: Chaplains facilitate communication between patients, families, and healthcare providers. They help families understand medical information, make informed decisions, and address any spiritual or ethical concerns that arise.

3. Grief and Bereavement Care: Chaplains support families through grief and bereavement, offering counseling, conducting memorial services, and providing resources for coping with loss. Their presence helps families find solace and meaning during difficult times.

Supporting Healthcare Staff:

1. Emotional and Moral Support: Chaplains offer emotional and moral support to healthcare staff, addressing the stress and challenges of working in a hospital environment. They provide a safe space for staff to express their feelings, discuss ethical dilemmas, and seek spiritual guidance.

2. Team Building and Resilience: Chaplains facilitate team-building activities and resilience training for healthcare staff. These initiatives foster a supportive work environment, enhance teamwork, and promote the well-being of staff members.

3. Ethical Consultations: Chaplains participate in ethical consultations, helping healthcare teams navigate complex ethical issues related to patient care. They offer insights from a spiritual and ethical perspective, contributing to informed and compassionate decision-making.

Conducting Religious and Spiritual Services:

1. Worship Services: Chaplains conduct regular worship services within the hospital, providing opportunities for patients, families, and staff to gather for communal worship, prayer, and reflection. These services foster a sense of community and spiritual connection.

2. Religious Observances: Chaplains organize and facilitate religious observances for various faith traditions, ensuring that patients can practice their faith during hospitalization. This includes arranging for dietary needs, observing religious holidays, and accommodating specific rituals.

3. Spiritual Resources: Chaplains provide spiritual resources, such as religious texts, prayer books, and devotional materials. These resources support patients and families in their spiritual practices and offer comfort during their hospital stay.

Addressing Ethical and Moral Issues:

1. Ethical Decision-Making: Chaplains assist patients, families, and healthcare providers in making ethical decisions related to medical care. They offer guidance on issues such as end-of-life care, informed consent, and advanced directives, helping individuals navigate moral complexities.

2. Advance Care Planning: Chaplains support patients and families in advance care planning, discussing preferences for medical treatment and end-of-life care. They facilitate conversations about values, beliefs, and goals, ensuring that patients' wishes are respected.

3. Conflict Resolution: Chaplains mediate conflicts that arise within the healthcare setting, whether between patients and families or within the healthcare team. They promote understanding, empathy, and resolution, fostering a collaborative and respectful environment.

The Impact of Chaplains in Hospitals

Enhancing Patient Well-Being: Chaplains contribute to patients' overall well-being by addressing their spiritual and emotional needs. Spiritual care can reduce anxiety, provide comfort, and improve patients' ability to cope with illness and treatment.

Supporting Family Coping: Chaplains play a crucial role in helping families cope with the stress and uncertainty of a loved one's hospitalization. Their support fosters resilience, facilitates informed decision-making, and promotes healing within the family unit.

Promoting Staff Resilience: By providing emotional and spiritual support to healthcare staff, chaplains enhance staff resilience and job satisfaction. This support helps reduce burnout, improve morale, and foster a positive work environment.

Facilitating Holistic Care: Chaplains integrate spiritual care into the broader healthcare team, promoting a holistic approach to patient care. This collaboration ensures that patients' spiritual, emotional, and physical needs are addressed comprehensively.

Contributing to Ethical Practices: Chaplains' involvement in ethical consultations and decision-making processes helps ensure that patient care is guided by ethical principles and compassionate practices. Their input promotes justice, respect, and dignity in medical care.

Case Studies in Hospital Chaplaincy

Supporting a Terminally Ill Patient:

Chaplain Emily was called to support Mr. Johnson, a terminally ill patient struggling with fear and anxiety about his impending death. Through regular visits, prayers, and spiritual conversations, Chaplain Emily helped Mr. Johnson find peace and acceptance. She also provided support to his family, helping them navigate their grief and prepare for his passing. Chaplain Emily's presence brought comfort and spiritual solace to Mr. Johnson and his loved ones during a difficult time.

Facilitating Ethical Decision-Making:

In a case involving a critically ill child, Chaplain James was asked to join an ethics consultation. The medical team and the child's parents faced a difficult decision about continuing life-sustaining treatment. Chaplain James facilitated a compassionate dialogue, helping the parents express their values and concerns. He offered spiritual support and ethical guidance, assisting the team in reaching a decision that respected the family's wishes and the child's best interests. Chaplain James' involvement ensured that the decision-making process was holistic and empathetic.

Promoting Staff Well-Being:

During a particularly challenging flu season, Chaplain Sarah noticed the increased stress and fatigue among the hospital staff. She organized weekly resilience workshops, including mindfulness exercises, stress management techniques, and spiritual reflections. These workshops provided staff members with tools to cope with the demands of their work and fostered a sense of community and mutual support. Chaplain Sarah's efforts contributed to improved staff morale and well-being during a taxing period.

Supporting a Family During Surgery:

When a young child required emergency surgery, Chaplain Michael provided support to the anxious parents. He stayed with them in the waiting room, offering prayers, listening to their fears, and providing updates from the surgical team. Chaplain Michael's compassionate presence helped the parents feel supported and less isolated during the critical hours. After the successful surgery, he continued to offer spiritual support, helping the family navigate the recovery process.

Challenges and Opportunities in Hospital Chaplaincy

Navigating Diverse Beliefs: One of the challenges chaplains face is navigating the diverse religious and spiritual beliefs of patients and families. Chaplains must be culturally competent and respectful, providing inclusive care that honors each individual's faith tradition.

Balancing Workload and Self-Care: The demands of hospital chaplaincy can be intense, with chaplains often working long hours and managing high caseloads. It is essential for chaplains to practice self-care and seek support to maintain their well-being and effectiveness.

Integrating into Healthcare Teams: Chaplains must work collaboratively with healthcare providers to integrate spiritual care into the overall treatment plan. Building strong relationships and effective communication within the healthcare team are crucial for holistic patient care.

Leveraging Technology: Advances in technology offer new opportunities for chaplains to provide spiritual support. Telechaplaincy and digital resources can extend the reach of chaplaincy services, offering support to patients and families who may not be able to receive in-person visits.

Chaplains in hospital settings play an essential role in providing holistic care that addresses the spiritual, emotional, and ethical needs of patients, families, and healthcare staff. Their presence and support enhance the overall quality of care, promoting well-being, resilience, and ethical integrity within the healthcare environment.

End-of-Life Care: Providing Spiritual and Emotional Support to Patients and Families During End-of-Life Situations

End-of-life care is a critical aspect of healthcare chaplaincy, where chaplains provide essential spiritual and emotional support to patients and their families as they navigate the profound and often challenging journey of approaching death. This chapter delves into the roles, responsibilities, and impact of chaplains in end-of-life care, illustrating how they help patients and families find peace, meaning, and comfort during this significant phase of life.

Understanding End-of-Life Care

Defining End-of-Life Care: End-of-life care involves the comprehensive support of patients who are nearing the end of their lives, addressing their physical, emotional, spiritual, and social needs. It also includes providing support to families as they cope with the impending loss of a loved one.

The Importance of Spiritual and Emotional Support: Spiritual and emotional support is vital in end-of-life care as it helps patients and families find meaning, reconcile unresolved issues, and experience a sense of peace. Chaplains play a crucial role in offering this support, helping individuals navigate their fears, hopes, and spiritual concerns.

The Role of Chaplains in End-of-Life Care

Providing Spiritual Care to Patients:

1. Presence and Listening: Chaplains offer a compassionate and non-judgmental presence, listening to patients' concerns, fears, and hopes. This presence provides comfort and allows patients to express their emotions and spiritual needs openly.

2. Prayer and Rituals: Chaplains lead patients in prayer and perform religious rituals, such as administering last rites,

anointing of the sick, or offering communion. These practices can provide profound spiritual comfort and a sense of peace.

3. Spiritual Counseling: Chaplains provide spiritual counseling to help patients explore and resolve spiritual or existential questions. This may involve discussing beliefs about life after death, seeking forgiveness, or finding meaning in their experiences.

Supporting Families:

1. Emotional Support: Chaplains provide emotional support to families, helping them cope with anticipatory grief, anxiety, and the stress of caregiving. They offer a listening ear, words of comfort, and practical guidance.

2. Facilitating Communication: Chaplains facilitate communication between patients, families, and healthcare providers. They help families understand medical information, discuss treatment options, and make informed decisions that align with the patient's wishes.

3. Bereavement Care: After a patient passes away, chaplains offer bereavement care to families, helping them navigate their grief and find ways to honor and remember their loved one. This includes conducting memorial services and providing resources for ongoing support.

Collaborating with Healthcare Teams:

1. Interdisciplinary Approach: Chaplains work as part of an interdisciplinary healthcare team, collaborating with doctors, nurses, social workers, and other professionals to provide holistic end-of-life care. They ensure that spiritual and emotional needs are integrated into the overall care plan.

2. Ethical Decision-Making: Chaplains assist in ethical decision-making processes, helping patients and families address complex issues such as advance directives, withdrawal of life-sustaining treatment, and palliative care options. They provide a moral and spiritual perspective that guides compassionate and respectful care.

3. Support for Healthcare Staff: Chaplains also provide support to healthcare staff, who may experience emotional and moral distress when caring for dying patients. They offer debriefing sessions, spiritual support, and resources to help staff cope with the demands of their work.

The Impact of Chaplaincy in End-of-Life Care

Enhancing Patient Well-Being: Chaplains contribute to the overall well-being of patients by addressing their spiritual and emotional needs. This support can reduce anxiety, alleviate spiritual distress, and help patients find peace and meaning as they approach the end of life.

Supporting Family Coping: Families benefit significantly from the support chaplains provide. Chaplains help families navigate their emotions, make important decisions, and prepare for the loss of their loved one, fostering resilience and healing.

Promoting Holistic Care: By integrating spiritual and emotional support into the healthcare team, chaplains promote a holistic approach to end-of-life care. This ensures that patients and families receive comprehensive care that addresses all aspects of their well-being.

Facilitating Ethical and Compassionate Decisions: Chaplains play a crucial role in facilitating ethical and compassionate decision-making. Their guidance helps ensure that care decisions respect the patient's values and wishes, promoting dignity and respect at the end of life.

Case Studies in End-of-Life Care

Providing Comfort During Terminal Illness:

Mr. Lee was a terminally ill patient with advanced cancer who struggled with intense fear and spiritual distress. Chaplain Angela visited him regularly, offering prayers, listening to his concerns, and discussing his beliefs about the afterlife. Through these conversations, Mr. Lee found comfort and a sense of peace, allowing him to face his remaining time with courage. Chaplain Angela also supported Mr. Lee's family, helping them cope with their grief and prepare for his passing.

Supporting a Family's Decision-Making Process:

Mrs. Hernandez was in the final stages of a chronic illness, and her family faced difficult decisions regarding her care. Chaplain Mark facilitated family meetings, providing a space for open and compassionate dialogue. He helped the family understand the medical options and discuss Mrs. Hernandez's wishes and values. With Chaplain Mark's support, the family decided to transition to palliative care, ensuring Mrs. Hernandez's comfort and dignity in her final days.

Guiding Ethical Discussions in a Hospital Setting:

In a busy hospital, Chaplain Sarah was called to support the family of an unconscious patient with no advance directives. The family was conflicted about whether to continue life-sustaining treatment. Chaplain Sarah guided the family through an ethical decision-making process, helping them consider the patient's previously expressed wishes, their own values, and the medical realities. Her compassionate guidance helped the family reach a consensus and make a decision that honored the patient's dignity.

Providing Bereavement Support:

After the sudden death of their loved one, the Thompson family was overwhelmed with grief. Chaplain James provided immediate support, offering prayers and words of comfort. He organized a memorial service that honored the deceased's life and faith, helping the family find closure. Chaplain James also connected the family with ongoing bereavement resources, ensuring they had continued support during their grieving process.

Challenges and Opportunities in End-of-Life Care

Navigating Diverse Beliefs: One of the challenges chaplains face is navigating the diverse religious and spiritual beliefs of patients and families. Chaplains must be culturally competent and respectful, providing care that honors each individual's faith tradition.

Addressing Emotional and Spiritual Distress: Patients and families often experience intense emotional and spiritual distress during end-of-life situations. Chaplains must be skilled in providing compassionate support, helping individuals process their emotions and find meaning and peace.

Balancing Clinical and Spiritual Roles: Chaplains work within clinical settings that prioritize medical treatment. Balancing their spiritual roles with the clinical environment requires effective communication and collaboration with healthcare teams to ensure holistic care.

Leveraging Technology: Advances in technology offer new opportunities for chaplains to provide end-of-life care. Telechaplaincy and digital resources can extend the reach of spiritual support, offering comfort to patients and families who may not be able to receive in-person visits.

End-of-life care is a crucial aspect of healthcare chaplaincy, where chaplains provide essential spiritual and emotional support to patients and families facing the profound challenges of approaching death. Through compassionate presence, prayer, spiritual counseling, and ethical guidance, chaplains help individuals find peace, meaning, and comfort during this significant phase of life.

Holistic Healing: Integrating Spiritual Care into the Broader Healthcare System

Holistic healing is a comprehensive approach to health and well-being that encompasses physical, emotional, mental, and spiritual dimensions. In the healthcare system, integrating spiritual care is essential for addressing the full spectrum of patient needs. This chapter explores the concept of holistic healing, the role of chaplains in promoting it, and the benefits of integrating spiritual care into the broader healthcare system.

Understanding Holistic Healing

Defining Holistic Healing: Holistic healing is an approach that considers the whole person—body, mind, spirit, and emotions—in the pursuit of optimal health and well-being. It emphasizes the interconnectedness of these dimensions and the importance of addressing all aspects of a person's life.

The Importance of Spiritual Care in Holistic Healing: Spiritual care is a critical component of holistic healing. It helps individuals find meaning, purpose, and connection, contributing to overall well-being. By addressing spiritual needs, healthcare providers can offer more comprehensive and compassionate care.

The Role of Chaplains in Promoting Holistic Healing Providing Spiritual Support:

1. Personalized Spiritual Care: Chaplains provide individualized spiritual care tailored to each patient's beliefs, values, and needs. This includes offering prayers, spiritual counseling, and rituals that resonate with the patient's faith tradition.

2. Listening and Presence: Chaplains offer a compassionate presence and active listening, allowing patients to express their fears, hopes, and spiritual concerns. This support helps patients feel understood and valued, enhancing their emotional and spiritual well-being.

3. Facilitating Spiritual Practices: Chaplains facilitate spiritual practices, such as meditation, prayer, and religious services, within the healthcare setting. These practices provide

comfort, promote relaxation, and foster a sense of connection and peace.

Supporting Emotional and Mental Health:

1. Counseling and Emotional Support: Chaplains provide counseling and emotional support to patients and families, helping them navigate the challenges of illness and hospitalization. This support addresses emotional distress, reduces anxiety, and promotes mental well-being.

2. Grief and Bereavement Care: Chaplains offer grief and bereavement support to individuals coping with loss. They provide counseling, conduct memorial services, and offer resources to help people process their grief and find healing.

3. Stress Reduction Techniques: Chaplains teach stress reduction techniques, such as mindfulness and relaxation exercises, that help patients manage stress and improve their overall well-being. These techniques promote mental clarity and emotional stability.

Collaborating with Healthcare Teams:

1. Interdisciplinary Collaboration: Chaplains work as part of an interdisciplinary healthcare team, collaborating with doctors, nurses, social workers, and other professionals to provide holistic care. This collaboration ensures that spiritual

and emotional needs are integrated into the overall treatment plan.

2. Ethical and Moral Support: Chaplains assist in ethical decision-making processes, providing a spiritual and moral perspective that guides compassionate and respectful care. They help patients, families, and healthcare providers navigate complex ethical issues.

3. Education and Training: Chaplains provide education and training to healthcare staff on the importance of spiritual care and holistic healing. This training enhances staff awareness and competence in addressing the spiritual needs of patients.

Benefits of Integrating Spiritual Care into Healthcare

Improved Patient Outcomes: Integrating spiritual care into healthcare can lead to improved patient outcomes, including reduced anxiety, depression, and pain. Patients who receive spiritual support often report higher levels of satisfaction and overall well-being.

Enhanced Coping Mechanisms: Spiritual care helps patients develop stronger coping mechanisms, enabling them to manage the stress and challenges of illness more effectively. It provides a source of strength, hope, and resilience.

Increased Patient Satisfaction: Patients who receive holistic care that includes spiritual support are more likely to feel understood, respected, and valued. This leads to increased patient satisfaction and a better healthcare experience.

Better Communication and Trust: Integrating spiritual care fosters better communication and trust between patients, families, and healthcare providers. It helps build a supportive and compassionate healthcare environment.

Comprehensive Care: By addressing the physical, emotional, mental, and spiritual dimensions of health, holistic care provides a more comprehensive approach to healing. It ensures that all aspects of a patient's well-being are considered and addressed.

Case Studies in Holistic Healing

Integrating Spiritual Care in Cancer Treatment:

In an oncology unit, Chaplain Laura collaborated with the medical team to integrate spiritual care into the treatment plans of cancer patients. She provided spiritual counseling, facilitated support groups, and conducted meditation sessions. Patients reported feeling more supported and hopeful, and many experienced reduced anxiety and improved emotional well-being. The integration of spiritual care enhanced the overall quality of life for these patients.

Holistic Care in Palliative Medicine:

Chaplain David worked in a palliative care unit, where he provided comprehensive spiritual support to patients with life-limiting illnesses. He conducted spiritual assessments, offered personalized prayers, and facilitated family meetings. By addressing spiritual concerns and providing emotional support, Chaplain David helped patients find peace and meaning in their final days. The holistic approach improved patient and family satisfaction with palliative care services.

Supporting Mental Health in Rehabilitation:

In a rehabilitation center, Chaplain Sarah integrated spiritual care into the treatment of patients recovering from substance abuse. She led spiritual reflection groups, offered individual counseling, and provided resources for spiritual growth. The patients benefited from the holistic approach, which addressed both their physical recovery and spiritual needs. Many reported enhanced motivation, better coping skills, and a stronger sense of purpose.

Collaborative Care in Intensive Care Units (ICUs):

Chaplain Michael collaborated with ICU staff to provide holistic care to critically ill patients. He offered spiritual support to patients and families, conducted ethical consultations, and participated in multidisciplinary rounds. By integrating spiritual care into the ICU, Chaplain Michael helped improve communication, reduce family stress, and support the emotional well-being of healthcare staff. The holistic approach contributed to a more compassionate and supportive ICU environment.

Challenges and Opportunities in Holistic Healing

Navigating Diverse Beliefs: One of the challenges in holistic healing is navigating the diverse religious and spiritual beliefs of patients. Chaplains must be culturally competent and respectful, providing inclusive care that honors each individual's faith tradition.

Balancing Clinical and Spiritual Roles: Chaplains work within clinical settings that prioritize medical treatment. Balancing their spiritual roles with the clinical environment requires effective communication and collaboration with healthcare teams to ensure holistic care.

Resource Limitations: Limited resources, such as time and staffing, can pose challenges to providing comprehensive spiritual care. Chaplains must advocate for the importance of spiritual care and seek support from healthcare administrators to integrate it effectively.

Leveraging Technology: Advances in technology offer new opportunities for integrating spiritual care into healthcare. Telechaplaincy and digital resources can extend the reach of spiritual support, offering comfort to patients and families who may not be able to receive in-person visits.

Holistic healing is an essential approach in healthcare that integrates spiritual care into the broader system, addressing the full spectrum of patient needs. Chaplains play a vital role in promoting holistic healing by providing spiritual support, emotional and mental health care, and collaborating with healthcare teams. Their work enhances patient outcomes, fosters better coping mechanisms, and ensures comprehensive care.

Case Studies: Real-Life Examples of Healthcare Chaplaincy Making a Difference

Healthcare chaplaincy is a field where the impact of spiritual care can be profoundly felt by patients, families, and healthcare staff. This chapter presents a series of case studies that illustrate how chaplains make a tangible difference in the lives of those they serve. These real-life examples highlight the diverse roles chaplains play and the meaningful outcomes that result from their work.

Case Study 1: Comforting a Terminally Ill Patient

Background: Mr. Johnson, a 68-year-old man with advanced cancer, was admitted to the hospital for palliative care. He struggled with intense fear and spiritual distress as he faced the end of his life.

Chaplain's Role: Chaplain Emily was assigned to support Mr. Johnson. She visited him regularly, offering a compassionate presence and listening to his concerns. She led him in prayer, discussed his beliefs about the afterlife, and performed the sacrament of anointing the sick.

Outcome: Through these interactions, Mr. Johnson found comfort and a sense of peace. He was able to express his fears and hopes, which alleviated much of his anxiety. His family also received support from Chaplain Emily, who helped them cope with their anticipatory grief. Mr. Johnson passed away peacefully, with his spiritual needs met and his family feeling supported.

Case Study 2: Navigating Ethical Dilemmas in ICU

Background: Mrs. Lee, a 45-year-old woman, was in the intensive care unit (ICU) after a severe stroke. Her prognosis was poor, and the family was faced with difficult decisions about continuing life-sustaining treatment.

Chaplain's Role: Chaplain James was called to provide support to Mrs. Lee's family. He facilitated family meetings, offering a space for open and compassionate dialogue. He helped the family understand the medical information, explore their values, and consider Mrs. Lee's previously expressed wishes.

Outcome: With Chaplain James' guidance, the family decided to transition to comfort care, respecting Mrs. Lee's wishes and values. The decision was made with a sense of peace and unity. Chaplain James continued to provide support, helping the family navigate their grief and honoring Mrs. Lee's life through a memorial service.

Case Study 3: Supporting Mental Health in Rehabilitation

Background: John, a 32-year-old recovering from substance abuse, was admitted to a rehabilitation center. He struggled with feelings of guilt, shame, and a lack of purpose.

Chaplain's Role: Chaplain Sarah provided spiritual counseling and facilitated support groups focused on spiritual reflection. She offered individual sessions where John could explore his feelings, seek forgiveness, and find spiritual strength. She also provided resources for meditation and prayer.

Outcome: John benefited significantly from the holistic approach. He reported enhanced motivation, better coping skills, and a stronger sense of purpose. Chaplain Sarah's support helped him reconnect with his faith, fostering a sense of hope and resilience in his recovery journey.

Case Study 4: Promoting Resilience Among Healthcare Staff

Background: During a particularly challenging flu season, the healthcare staff at a hospital experienced increased stress and fatigue. The emotional toll was evident, with many staff members feeling overwhelmed.

Chaplain's Role: Chaplain David organized weekly resilience workshops for the staff, including mindfulness exercises, stress management techniques, and spiritual reflections. He also provided one-on-one support sessions for those in need of additional care.

Outcome: The resilience workshops were highly appreciated by the staff. Participants reported feeling more supported and better equipped to manage stress. The overall morale and well-being of the healthcare team improved, demonstrating the positive impact of Chaplain David's initiatives.

Case Study 5: Supporting a Family During Pediatric Surgery

Background: The Garcia family faced the anxiety of their 5-year-old daughter, Maria, undergoing a major surgery. The family was deeply distressed, struggling with fear and uncertainty.

Chaplain's Role: Chaplain Mark provided continuous support to the Garcia family. He stayed with them in the waiting room, offering prayers and listening to their concerns. He also communicated with the surgical team to provide updates and facilitated moments of prayer and reflection.

Outcome: Chaplain Mark's presence helped the Garcia family feel less isolated and more supported. His compassionate care provided emotional stability during the surgery. Following the successful operation, he continued to offer spiritual support, helping the family navigate the recovery process with a renewed sense of hope and gratitude.

Case Study 6: Addressing Grief in a Hospice Setting

Background: Mrs. Thompson was in hospice care, approaching the end of her life due to terminal illness. Her family was overwhelmed with grief and uncertainty about how to cope with the impending loss.

Chaplain's Role: Chaplain Lisa provided ongoing spiritual and emotional support to both Mrs. Thompson and her family. She facilitated conversations about end-of-life wishes, provided counseling, and led prayer sessions. She also organized a bedside vigil and coordinated a memorial service.

Outcome: Chaplain Lisa's support helped Mrs. Thompson find peace and comfort in her final days. Her family felt supported and better prepared to cope with their grief. The memorial service provided a meaningful way to honor Mrs. Thompson's life, bringing a sense of closure and healing to the family.

These case studies highlight the profound and varied impact of healthcare chaplaincy. Chaplains provide critical spiritual, emotional, and ethical support in diverse healthcare settings, addressing the holistic needs of patients, families, and healthcare staff. Through compassionate presence, prayer, counseling, and ethical guidance, chaplains make a significant difference in the lives of those they serve.

CHAPTER 05

CORPORATE CHAPLAINCY

Workplace Spirituality: The Rise of Spiritual Care in Corporate Environments

Workplace spirituality has emerged as a significant aspect of corporate chaplaincy, addressing the spiritual, emotional, and ethical needs of employees within the corporate environment. As companies recognize the importance of holistic well-being, the role of chaplains in the workplace has expanded. This chapter explores the rise of workplace spirituality, the functions of corporate chaplains, and the impact of their work on employees and organizations.

Understanding Workplace Spirituality

Defining Workplace Spirituality: Workplace spirituality involves creating a work environment that supports the spiritual and emotional well-being of employees. It emphasizes meaning, purpose, and connection, encouraging a sense of community and ethical integrity within the workplace.

The Importance of Spiritual Care in Corporate Settings: Spiritual care in corporate settings enhances employee well-being, improves morale, and fosters a positive organizational culture. By addressing spiritual needs, companies can promote holistic health, reduce stress, and increase employee engagement and productivity.

The Role of Corporate Chaplains

Providing Spiritual Support:

1. Individual Counseling: Corporate chaplains offer confidential counseling sessions to employees, addressing personal and professional concerns. These sessions provide a safe space for employees to discuss their struggles, seek guidance, and find spiritual comfort.

2. Prayer and Meditation: Chaplains facilitate prayer and meditation sessions, helping employees find peace and clarity amidst the pressures of the workplace. These practices promote relaxation, reduce stress, and enhance overall well-being.

3. Spiritual Resources: Chaplains provide spiritual resources, such as inspirational literature, prayer books, and guided meditations. These resources support employees in their personal spiritual practices and offer encouragement during challenging times.

Fostering Community and Connection:

1. Group Activities: Chaplains organize group activities, such as prayer groups, discussion circles, and spiritual retreats. These activities foster a sense of community and mutual support, helping employees build meaningful relationships.

2. Workplace Rituals: Chaplains lead workplace rituals that mark significant events, such as the beginning of a new project, milestones, or the passing of a colleague. These rituals provide a sense of continuity and connection, enhancing the workplace culture.

3. Team Building: Chaplains facilitate team-building exercises that promote trust, collaboration, and a sense of shared purpose. These activities strengthen interpersonal relationships and improve team dynamics.

Promoting Ethical Integrity:

1. Ethical Counseling: Chaplains provide ethical counseling, helping employees navigate moral dilemmas and uphold their values in the workplace. They offer guidance on issues such as honesty, fairness, and ethical decision-making.

2. Ethical Training: Chaplains conduct ethical training sessions, educating employees about the importance of integrity and ethical behavior. These sessions promote a culture of accountability and respect within the organization.

3. Conflict Resolution: Chaplains assist in resolving workplace conflicts by facilitating open and respectful dialogue. They help employees understand different perspectives, find common ground, and develop solutions that align with ethical principles.

Supporting Organizational Well-Being:

1. Wellness Programs: Chaplains contribute to wellness programs that address the physical, emotional, and spiritual health of employees. These programs include stress management workshops, mindfulness training, and wellness retreats.

2. Leadership Support: Chaplains provide support to corporate leaders, helping them navigate the challenges of leadership with integrity and compassion. They offer guidance on maintaining ethical standards, fostering a positive work environment, and supporting employee well-being.

3. Crisis Management: Chaplains play a crucial role in crisis management, offering support during times of organizational change, layoffs, or traumatic events. They

provide counseling, facilitate support groups, and help employees cope with the emotional impact of crises.

The Impact of Workplace Spirituality

Enhanced Employee Well-Being: Integrating spiritual care into the workplace enhances employee well-being by addressing their holistic needs. Employees who receive spiritual support report lower levels of stress, higher job satisfaction, and improved mental health.

Increased Employee Engagement: Workplace spirituality fosters a sense of meaning and purpose, increasing employee engagement and motivation. Employees who feel connected to their work and supported in their spiritual journey are more likely to be productive and committed to the organization.

Improved Organizational Culture: Chaplains contribute to a positive organizational culture by promoting ethical behavior, fostering community, and supporting employee well-being. A culture of integrity, respect, and mutual support enhances overall organizational health.

Strengthened Leadership: Leaders who receive spiritual and ethical support from chaplains are better equipped to lead with compassion and integrity. This strengthens their ability to inspire and motivate employees, fostering a positive and productive work environment.

Better Crisis Management: During times of crisis, chaplains provide essential support that helps employees cope and recover. Their presence and guidance help mitigate the emotional impact of crises, promoting resilience and stability within the organization.

Case Studies in Workplace Spirituality

Supporting Employees During Organizational Change:

At a large corporation undergoing significant restructuring, Chaplain Laura provided crucial support to employees facing uncertainty and stress. She organized prayer and meditation sessions, facilitated support groups, and offered individual counseling. Her efforts helped employees navigate the changes with greater resilience and trust in the organization's future.

Promoting Ethical Integrity in a Financial Firm:

Chaplain David worked with a financial firm to promote ethical behavior and integrity. He conducted ethical training sessions, provided counseling on ethical dilemmas, and facilitated discussions on the importance of honesty and transparency. As a result, the firm saw a decrease in unethical practices and an increase in employee trust and accountability.

Fostering Community in a Tech Company:

At a fast-growing tech company, Chaplain Sarah focused on building a sense of community among employees. She organized weekly discussion circles, spiritual retreats, and team-building activities. These initiatives fostered stronger relationships, improved collaboration, and enhanced the overall workplace culture.

Crisis Management in a Manufacturing Plant:

After a tragic accident at a manufacturing plant, Chaplain Mark provided immediate and ongoing support to employees. He offered grief counseling, facilitated memorial services, and helped the organization develop a comprehensive crisis management plan. His presence and guidance were instrumental in helping employees cope with the trauma and rebuild a sense of normalcy.

Challenges and Opportunities in Workplace Spirituality

Navigating Diverse Beliefs: One of the challenges in promoting workplace spirituality is navigating the diverse religious and spiritual beliefs of employees. Chaplains must be culturally competent and inclusive, providing support that respects and honors each individual's faith tradition.

Balancing Personal and Professional Roles: Chaplains must balance their personal spiritual beliefs with their professional roles, ensuring that their support is inclusive and non-proselytizing. This requires sensitivity, humility, and a commitment to respecting the beliefs of others.

Resource Limitations: Limited resources, such as time and funding, can pose challenges to implementing comprehensive spiritual care programs. Chaplains must advocate for the importance of spiritual care and seek support from corporate leaders to integrate it effectively.

Leveraging Technology: Advances in technology offer new opportunities for promoting workplace spirituality. Virtual chaplaincy services, online support groups, and digital resources can extend the reach of spiritual care, offering support to employees regardless of location.

Workplace spirituality is a vital aspect of corporate chaplaincy, addressing the spiritual, emotional, and ethical needs of employees within the corporate environment. By providing spiritual support, fostering community, promoting ethical integrity, and supporting organizational well-being, chaplains play a crucial role in enhancing the overall health and productivity of the workplace.

Employee Support: How Chaplains Assist Employees with Personal and Professional Challenges

In today's fast-paced and demanding work environments, employees often face a myriad of personal and professional challenges. Corporate chaplains play a crucial role in providing support that addresses these issues, fostering a healthier, more productive workplace. This chapter explores how chaplains assist employees in navigating both personal and professional challenges, highlighting their methods and the impact of their work.

Understanding the Role of Chaplains in Employee Support

Defining Employee Support: Employee support in the context of chaplaincy involves offering spiritual, emotional, and practical assistance to employees facing a variety of challenges. This support aims to improve well-being, enhance job satisfaction, and foster a positive workplace culture.

The Importance of Chaplaincy in the Workplace: Chaplains provide a unique form of support that complements other employee assistance programs. By addressing the holistic needs of employees, chaplains help individuals find balance, meaning, and resilience, ultimately contributing to a more engaged and productive workforce.

Methods of Supporting Employees

Providing Personal Support:

1. Confidential Counseling: Chaplains offer confidential one-on-one counseling sessions, providing a safe

space for employees to discuss personal issues such as stress, family problems, grief, and mental health concerns. These sessions help employees process their emotions and develop coping strategies.

2. Spiritual Guidance: Chaplains provide spiritual guidance tailored to the individual's beliefs and values. This may include prayer, meditation, or discussions about faith and spirituality, helping employees find comfort and direction during difficult times.

3. Crisis Intervention: In times of personal crisis, such as the death of a loved one, divorce, or serious illness, chaplains provide immediate support and ongoing care. They offer a compassionate presence, helping employees navigate their grief and begin the healing process.

Supporting Professional Development:

1. Career Counseling: Chaplains assist employees with professional challenges, offering career counseling and advice on navigating workplace dynamics. They help individuals identify their strengths, set career goals, and develop strategies for achieving them.

2. Conflict Resolution: Chaplains mediate workplace conflicts, facilitating open and respectful communication between parties. They help employees understand different

perspectives, resolve disputes, and restore positive working relationships.

3. Ethical Guidance: Chaplains provide guidance on ethical dilemmas, helping employees align their professional actions with their personal values. This support fosters a culture of integrity and ethical behavior within the organization.

Enhancing Emotional Well-Being:

1. Stress Management: Chaplains offer stress management techniques, such as mindfulness exercises, relaxation methods, and time management strategies. These practices help employees manage work-related stress and maintain emotional balance.

2. Support Groups: Chaplains facilitate support groups where employees can share their experiences and offer mutual support. These groups provide a sense of community and belonging, reducing feelings of isolation and promoting collective resilience.

3. Work-Life Balance: Chaplains help employees achieve a better work-life balance by offering advice on managing personal and professional responsibilities. They encourage practices that promote well-being, such as setting boundaries and prioritizing self-care.

Promoting Holistic Health:

1. Wellness Programs: Chaplains contribute to wellness programs that address the physical, emotional, and spiritual health of employees. These programs include workshops on healthy living, mental health awareness, and spiritual practices.

2. Resource Provision: Chaplains provide resources such as literature, referrals to external services, and access to spiritual materials. These resources support employees in their personal and professional development.

3. Celebrating Milestones: Chaplains recognize and celebrate important milestones in employees' lives, such as birthdays, work anniversaries, and personal achievements. This acknowledgment fosters a positive and supportive workplace environment.

Case Studies in Employee Support

Supporting an Employee Through Grief:

When John, an employee at a large corporation, lost his spouse unexpectedly, he struggled to cope with his grief while managing his work responsibilities. Chaplain Emily provided immediate support, offering a listening ear and comforting presence. She arranged for grief counseling sessions and facilitated a support group for employees experiencing loss. With Chaplain Emily's guidance, John found a safe space to express his emotions and received the support he needed to begin healing.

Navigating Workplace Conflict:

In a financial firm, two employees, Sarah and Mike, were in constant conflict, affecting their productivity and team dynamics. Chaplain David stepped in to mediate the situation. He facilitated several mediation sessions, helping Sarah and Mike communicate openly and respectfully. Through these discussions, they identified the root causes of their conflict and developed strategies to work together more effectively. Chaplain David's intervention restored a positive working relationship and improved the overall team morale.

Career Counseling and Professional Growth:

Maria, an employee at a tech company, felt stuck in her career and uncertain about her professional future. She sought guidance from Chaplain James, who provided career counseling and helped her assess her strengths and goals. Together, they developed a career plan that included further education and skill development. Chaplain James also provided ongoing support and encouragement as Maria pursued new opportunities. As a result, Maria gained confidence and clarity in her career path, leading to greater job satisfaction and professional growth.

Supporting Mental Health:

At a high-stress law firm, many employees were experiencing burnout and mental health challenges. Chaplain Lisa introduced a series of mental health workshops, focusing on stress management, mindfulness, and work-life balance. She also provided individual counseling sessions for employees needing additional support. These initiatives helped employees develop better coping mechanisms, reduced overall stress levels, and fostered a more supportive work environment.

Crisis Intervention:

Following a sudden downsizing at a manufacturing plant, many employees were left anxious and uncertain about their futures. Chaplain Mark provided immediate crisis intervention, offering individual counseling and organizing support groups to address the collective anxiety. He also worked with the management to ensure transparent communication and offered resources for those seeking new employment. Chaplain Mark's efforts helped stabilize the emotional climate and provided a sense of hope and direction during a challenging transition.

The Impact of Chaplaincy on Employee Well-Being

Enhanced Emotional Well-Being: Employees who receive chaplaincy support report lower levels of stress, anxiety, and depression. Chaplains provide tools and resources that help employees manage their emotions and maintain mental health.

Improved Job Satisfaction: Chaplains help create a supportive and positive work environment, leading to higher job satisfaction. Employees feel valued and understood, which enhances their commitment to the organization.

Increased Productivity: By addressing personal and professional challenges, chaplains help employees stay focused and productive. Supportive interventions reduce distractions and enable employees to perform at their best.

Stronger Workplace Relationships: Chaplain-led initiatives, such as conflict resolution and team-building activities, foster stronger interpersonal relationships. Employees develop better communication skills and a sense of camaraderie.

Holistic Health and Well-Being: Chaplains promote holistic health, addressing the physical, emotional, mental, and spiritual needs of employees. This comprehensive approach leads to overall well-being and a healthier workforce.

Challenges and Opportunities in Employee Support

Navigating Confidentiality: Maintaining confidentiality is crucial in chaplaincy. Chaplains must ensure that employees feel safe discussing personal issues without fear of repercussions.

Balancing Diverse Needs: Chaplains must balance the diverse spiritual and emotional needs of a multicultural workforce. Providing inclusive support that respects all beliefs and values is essential.

Resource Allocation: Limited resources, such as time and funding, can pose challenges. Chaplains must advocate for the importance of their role and seek support from corporate leadership to effectively meet employees' needs.

Leveraging Technology: Technology offers opportunities to extend chaplaincy services, such as through virtual counseling and online support groups. Utilizing digital tools can enhance the accessibility and reach of chaplaincy support.

Chaplains play a vital role in supporting employees through personal and professional challenges, offering a unique blend of spiritual, emotional, and practical assistance. By providing confidential counseling, spiritual guidance, crisis intervention, and promoting holistic health, chaplains enhance the overall well-being and productivity of the workforce.

Ethical Leadership: Promoting Ethical Behavior and Corporate Responsibility Through Chaplaincy

In the corporate world, ethical leadership is crucial for maintaining integrity, building trust, and fostering a positive organizational culture. Corporate chaplains play a significant role in promoting ethical behavior and corporate responsibility. This chapter explores how chaplains influence ethical leadership, the strategies they use, and the impact of their work on organizations.

Understanding Ethical Leadership

Defining Ethical Leadership: Ethical leadership involves guiding and influencing others to act with integrity, fairness, and respect. Ethical leaders prioritize ethical standards, transparency, and accountability in their decision-making processes and interactions with others.

The Importance of Ethical Leadership in Corporations: Ethical leadership is essential for building a trustworthy and reputable organization. It fosters a culture of integrity, promotes ethical behavior, and enhances the overall sustainability of the business. Ethical leaders inspire employees, strengthen stakeholder relationships, and contribute to long-term success.

The Role of Chaplains in Promoting Ethical Leadership

Providing Ethical Guidance:

1. Confidential Counseling: Chaplains offer confidential counseling to leaders and employees, helping

them navigate ethical dilemmas and make decisions that align with their values and the organization's ethical standards. These sessions provide a safe space for individuals to discuss their concerns and seek guidance.

2. Ethical Decision-Making Support: Chaplains assist in the decision-making process by providing a moral and ethical perspective. They help leaders consider the ethical implications of their actions, ensuring that decisions are made with integrity and fairness.

3. Moral Reflection: Chaplains facilitate moral reflection, encouraging leaders to reflect on their actions and the ethical principles that guide them. This practice helps leaders stay true to their values and promotes continuous ethical growth.

Fostering a Culture of Integrity:

1. Ethical Training and Workshops: Chaplains conduct ethical training sessions and workshops, educating employees and leaders on the importance of ethical behavior and corporate responsibility. These programs cover topics such as ethical decision-making, conflict resolution, and corporate social responsibility.

2. Ethical Communication: Chaplains promote open and honest communication within the organization. They

encourage leaders to be transparent about their decisions and to communicate ethical standards clearly to all employees.

3. Ethical Policies and Practices: Chaplains work with leadership to develop and implement ethical policies and practices. These policies provide a framework for ethical behavior and ensure that the organization operates with integrity and accountability.

Supporting Corporate Responsibility:

1. Community Engagement: Chaplains encourage and support corporate social responsibility initiatives. They help organizations develop programs that give back to the community, promote sustainability, and address social and environmental issues.

2. Ethical Business Practices: Chaplains advocate for ethical business practices that prioritize fairness, respect, and social responsibility. They support initiatives that promote fair trade, ethical sourcing, and responsible marketing.

3. Stakeholder Relationships: Chaplains help leaders build and maintain ethical relationships with stakeholders, including employees, customers, suppliers, and the community. They promote transparency, accountability, and mutual respect in all interactions.

Promoting Ethical Behavior:

1. Role Modeling: Chaplains serve as role models for ethical behavior. Their actions and interactions demonstrate

the importance of integrity, compassion, and respect, inspiring others to follow their example.

2. Conflict Resolution: Chaplains mediate conflicts and address unethical behavior within the organization. They facilitate open discussions, help individuals understand different perspectives, and promote resolutions that align with ethical principles.

3. Recognition and Reward: Chaplains advocate for recognizing and rewarding ethical behavior. They support initiatives that celebrate individuals and teams who demonstrate integrity and contribute positively to the organization's ethical culture.

The Impact of Ethical Leadership on Organizations

Enhanced Reputation and Trust: Organizations that prioritize ethical leadership build a strong reputation and earn the trust of stakeholders. This trust translates into customer loyalty, employee engagement, and positive relationships with the community.

Increased Employee Engagement: Ethical leadership fosters a positive work environment where employees feel valued and respected. Engaged employees are more productive, committed, and motivated to contribute to the organization's success.

Improved Decision-Making: Ethical leaders make decisions that consider the long-term impact on all stakeholders. This approach leads to more sustainable and responsible business practices, reducing risks and enhancing overall performance.

Stronger Corporate Culture: A culture of integrity and ethical behavior promotes collaboration, innovation, and a sense of shared purpose. Organizations with strong ethical cultures are better equipped to navigate challenges and seize opportunities.

Positive Social Impact: Organizations that embrace corporate responsibility initiatives contribute positively to society. These efforts enhance the organization's reputation, create goodwill, and make a meaningful difference in the communities they serve.

Case Studies in Ethical Leadership

Promoting Transparency in Financial Reporting:

At a large financial institution, Chaplain Laura worked closely with the leadership team to promote transparency and ethical practices in financial reporting. She conducted workshops on ethical decision-making, facilitated discussions on the importance of honesty and integrity, and provided confidential counseling to leaders facing ethical dilemmas. As a result, the organization saw an improvement in the accuracy and transparency of its financial reports, building trust with stakeholders and enhancing its reputation.

Supporting Ethical Sourcing Practices:

Chaplain David partnered with a manufacturing company to support ethical sourcing practices. He helped develop policies that prioritized fair labor practices, environmentally sustainable sourcing, and supplier accountability. Through ethical training sessions and continuous support, Chaplain David ensured that the company's sourcing practices aligned with its commitment to corporate responsibility. The company's ethical sourcing initiatives strengthened its brand reputation and fostered positive relationships with suppliers and customers.

Addressing Workplace Harassment:

In a tech company, Chaplain Sarah addressed issues of workplace harassment by promoting a culture of respect and accountability. She conducted training sessions on ethical behavior and conflict resolution, provided confidential support to affected employees, and worked with leadership to implement policies that prevented harassment and supported victims. Chaplain Sarah's efforts led to a significant reduction in harassment incidents and created a safer, more respectful work environment.

Enhancing Community Engagement:

Chaplain James helped a retail corporation enhance its community engagement initiatives. He collaborated with leadership to develop programs that addressed local needs, such as supporting education, promoting environmental sustainability, and providing resources for underserved communities. Chaplain James also organized volunteer opportunities for employees, fostering a sense of purpose and community involvement. The corporation's enhanced community engagement efforts improved its public image and created a positive social impact.

Building Ethical Leadership in Healthcare:

At a healthcare organization, Chaplain Mark focused on building ethical leadership among medical professionals. He provided ethical counseling to healthcare leaders, facilitated discussions on ethical challenges in patient care, and promoted policies that prioritized patient rights and well-being. Chaplain Mark's work helped create a culture of ethical care, improving patient satisfaction and trust in the organization.

Challenges and Opportunities in Promoting Ethical Leadership

Navigating Complex Ethical Dilemmas: Ethical dilemmas in corporate settings can be complex and multifaceted. Chaplains must navigate these challenges with sensitivity and wisdom, providing clear and compassionate guidance.

Balancing Profit and Responsibility: Organizations often face the challenge of balancing profitability with ethical responsibility. Chaplains play a crucial role in advocating for ethical practices that align with long-term success and sustainability.

Fostering Ethical Leadership at All Levels: Promoting ethical leadership requires a commitment from all levels of the organization, from top executives to front-line employees. Chaplains work to inspire and support ethical behavior across the entire organization.

Leveraging Technology for Ethical Training: Advances in technology offer new opportunities for ethical training and support. Virtual workshops, online resources, and digital communication tools can enhance the reach and impact of chaplaincy services.

Building a Culture of Continuous Improvement: Ethical leadership is an ongoing process that requires continuous reflection and improvement. Chaplains support organizations in maintaining a commitment to ethical growth and development.

Ethical leadership is a cornerstone of successful and responsible organizations. Corporate chaplains play a vital role in promoting ethical behavior and corporate responsibility by providing ethical guidance, fostering a culture of integrity, supporting corporate responsibility initiatives, and promoting ethical behavior.

Success Stories: Instances of Corporate Chaplaincy Fostering a Positive Workplace Culture

Corporate chaplaincy has proven to be a transformative element in creating and maintaining a positive workplace culture. By providing spiritual, emotional, and ethical support, chaplains enhance the overall well-being of employees and promote a culture of respect, integrity, and collaboration. This chapter highlights several success stories where corporate chaplaincy has made a significant impact on workplace culture.

Success Story 1: Enhancing Employee Morale and Engagement

Company: Tech Innovators Inc.

Challenge: Tech Innovators Inc. faced low employee morale and engagement due to high workloads and a fast-paced environment. Employees reported feeling stressed, undervalued, and disconnected from their work.

Chaplain's Role: Chaplain Emily was brought in to address these issues. She conducted regular one-on-one counseling sessions, organized mindfulness and relaxation workshops, and facilitated team-building activities. She also introduced weekly reflection meetings where employees could share their experiences and support one another.

Outcome: Over six months, employee morale and engagement improved significantly. Employees reported feeling more valued and connected to their work. The mindfulness workshops helped reduce stress levels, and the team-building activities fostered a sense of community and collaboration. Chaplain Emily's presence and initiatives played a crucial role in transforming the workplace culture into a more positive and supportive environment.

Success Story 2: Promoting Ethical Behavior and Integrity

Company: Global Finance Solutions

Challenge: Global Finance Solutions was struggling with issues related to unethical behavior and a lack of transparency. There were reports of dishonesty and conflicts of interest, which eroded trust among employees and with clients.

Chaplain's Role: Chaplain David introduced a comprehensive ethical training program that included workshops on integrity, transparency, and ethical decision-making. He also provided confidential counseling to employees facing ethical dilemmas and facilitated open discussions about the importance of ethical behavior.

Outcome: Within a year, there was a noticeable improvement in ethical behavior and transparency within the organization. Employees became more aware of the ethical standards expected of them and were more confident in addressing and reporting unethical practices. The culture of integrity and accountability fostered by Chaplain David helped rebuild trust among employees and clients, enhancing the company's reputation and performance.

Success Story 3: Supporting Mental Health and Well-Being

Company: HealthCare Plus

Challenge: HealthCare Plus, a large healthcare provider, was experiencing high levels of burnout and mental health issues among its staff. The demanding nature of healthcare work, combined with long hours and emotional stress, was taking a toll on employees.

Chaplain's Role: Chaplain Sarah implemented a mental health support program that included regular counseling sessions, stress management workshops, and resilience training. She also organized support groups where healthcare professionals could share their experiences and receive peer support.

Outcome: The mental health support program led to a significant reduction in burnout and stress levels among staff. Employees felt better equipped to handle the demands of their work and appreciated the opportunity to discuss their challenges in a supportive environment. Chaplain Sarah's efforts created a culture of care and compassion, improving overall job satisfaction and retention rates.

Success Story 4: Building Community and Collaboration

Company: GreenTech Manufacturing

Challenge: GreenTech Manufacturing faced issues with siloed departments and a lack of communication and collaboration across teams. This led to inefficiencies and a fragmented workplace culture.

Chaplain's Role: Chaplain James introduced initiatives to break down silos and promote collaboration. He organized cross-departmental workshops, facilitated interdepartmental projects, and held regular community-building events. He also provided a platform for employees to share ideas and collaborate on solutions to common challenges.

Outcome: The initiatives led to improved communication and collaboration across departments. Employees began to see the value of working together and sharing knowledge. The community-building events fostered stronger relationships and a sense of unity within the company. Chaplain James's efforts transformed GreenTech Manufacturing into a more cohesive and efficient organization.

Success Story 5: Navigating Organizational Change

Company: Retail Dynamics

Challenge: Retail Dynamics was undergoing significant organizational changes, including a major restructuring and the introduction of new technologies. These changes created uncertainty and anxiety among employees.

Chaplain's Role: Chaplain Mark provided support to employees during this transition by offering counseling, facilitating change management workshops, and maintaining open lines of communication. He organized forums where employees could express their concerns and ask questions about the changes.

Outcome: Chaplain Mark's support helped employees navigate the changes with greater confidence and less anxiety. The change management workshops equipped employees with the skills to adapt to new processes and technologies. The open forums fostered transparency and trust between management and staff. Chaplain Mark's efforts ensured a smoother transition and helped maintain morale and productivity during a challenging period.

Success Story 6: Enhancing Diversity and Inclusion

Company: InnovateCorp

Challenge: InnovateCorp was struggling with diversity and inclusion issues, leading to a lack of representation and feelings of exclusion among minority groups within the company.

Chaplain's Role: Chaplain Lisa worked with the company's leadership to develop and implement diversity and inclusion initiatives. She facilitated diversity training programs, organized cultural awareness events, and provided support to employee resource groups. She also offered counseling to individuals facing discrimination or bias.

Outcome: The diversity and inclusion initiatives led to a more inclusive and welcoming workplace culture. Employees from diverse backgrounds felt more valued and included. The cultural awareness events promoted understanding and respect among all employees. Chaplain Lisa's efforts helped InnovateCorp become a more diverse and inclusive organization, enhancing creativity, innovation, and employee satisfaction.

These success stories demonstrate the profound impact corporate chaplaincy can have on fostering a positive workplace culture. By addressing a wide range of challenges—from ethical behavior and mental health to collaboration and diversity—chaplains play a crucial role in enhancing the well-being and effectiveness of organizations.

CHAPTER 06

EDUCATIONAL CHAPLAINCY

Role in Schools: The Importance of Chaplains in Primary, Secondary, and Higher Education

Educational chaplaincy plays a vital role in fostering the spiritual, emotional, and ethical well-being of students, staff, and faculty across various educational settings. From primary schools to universities, chaplains provide essential support that enhances the educational environment and contributes to holistic development. This chapter explores the diverse roles and impact of chaplains in primary, secondary, and higher education.

Understanding Educational Chaplaincy

Defining Educational Chaplaincy: Educational chaplaincy involves providing spiritual, emotional, and ethical support within educational institutions. Chaplains address the needs of students, staff, and faculty, promoting well-being, ethical behavior, and a positive school culture.

The Importance of Chaplaincy in Education: Chaplains contribute to the holistic development of individuals in educational settings. They support academic and personal growth, foster a sense of community, and help navigate the challenges and pressures associated with education.

The Role of Chaplains in Primary and Secondary Schools

Providing Spiritual and Emotional Support:

1. Pastoral Care: Chaplains offer pastoral care to students, providing a compassionate presence and listening ear. They help students navigate personal challenges, such as family issues, bullying, and mental health concerns, offering guidance and support.

2. Spiritual Development: Chaplains facilitate spiritual development through activities such as prayer, meditation, and religious education. They help students explore and understand their faith, fostering spiritual growth and resilience.

3. Crisis Intervention: In times of crisis, such as the loss of a loved one or a school-wide emergency, chaplains provide immediate and ongoing support. They offer counseling, lead memorial services, and help the school community process and heal from the trauma.

Promoting Ethical Behavior and Character Development:

1. Ethical Education: Chaplains conduct ethical education programs, teaching students about values such as honesty, respect, and compassion. These programs encourage students to develop strong moral character and make ethical decisions.

2. Conflict Resolution: Chaplains mediate conflicts between students, helping them resolve disputes peacefully and respectfully. They teach conflict resolution skills, promoting a culture of understanding and cooperation.

3. Role Modeling: Chaplains serve as role models for ethical behavior. Their actions and interactions demonstrate the importance of integrity, empathy, and respect, inspiring students to emulate these qualities.

Fostering a Positive School Culture:

1. Community Building: Chaplains organize activities that foster a sense of community within the school. These

activities include school-wide assemblies, service projects, and cultural events that bring students, staff, and families together.

2. Support for Staff and Faculty: Chaplains provide support to teachers and staff, helping them manage stress and maintain their well-being. They offer counseling, lead staff retreats, and create opportunities for professional and personal development.

3. Inclusive Environment: Chaplains promote inclusivity and respect for diversity within the school community. They support initiatives that celebrate different cultures, religions, and backgrounds, fostering a welcoming and respectful environment for all.

The Role of Chaplains in Higher Education

Supporting Students' Academic and Personal Growth:

1. Counseling Services: Chaplains offer counseling services to college and university students, addressing academic pressures, mental health issues, and personal challenges. They provide a safe space for students to express their concerns and find support.

2. Spiritual Enrichment: Chaplains facilitate spiritual enrichment activities, such as religious services, meditation sessions, and faith-based discussions. These activities help students explore their spirituality and find balance amidst the demands of higher education.

3. Mentorship: Chaplains serve as mentors, guiding students through their academic and personal journeys. They offer advice on managing stress, making ethical decisions, and finding purpose and meaning in their studies and lives.

Enhancing Campus Community and Inclusivity:

1. Interfaith Dialogue: Chaplains promote interfaith dialogue and understanding on campus. They organize interfaith events, panel discussions, and collaborative projects that encourage students from different faith backgrounds to learn from and support one another.

2. Community Service: Chaplains lead community service initiatives, encouraging students to engage in volunteer work and social justice projects. These activities foster a sense of social responsibility and connection to the broader community.

3. Support for Marginalized Groups: Chaplains provide targeted support to marginalized and underrepresented groups on campus. They advocate for inclusivity, offer specialized counseling, and create safe spaces for these students to share their experiences and find solidarity.

Contributing to Ethical Leadership and Civic Engagement:

1. Ethics Education: Chaplains conduct ethics education programs that prepare students for leadership roles. These programs cover topics such as ethical decision-making, civic responsibility, and social justice, empowering students to act with integrity and compassion in their future careers.

2. Leadership Development: Chaplains support leadership development by mentoring student leaders and facilitating leadership training programs. They help students develop the skills and values needed to lead effectively and ethically.

3. Civic Engagement: Chaplains encourage civic engagement by organizing events and activities that connect students with local and global issues. They inspire students to take an active role in their communities and contribute positively to society.

Case Studies in Educational Chaplaincy

Supporting Mental Health in a High School:

At a high school, Chaplain Lisa noticed increasing levels of stress and anxiety among students, particularly during exam periods. She introduced a series of mindfulness workshops and stress management sessions, providing students with practical tools to manage their anxiety. She also offered individual counseling and created a peer support group. As a result, students reported feeling more equipped to handle stress, and the overall mental health of the student body improved.

Promoting Ethical Behavior in a Middle School:

Chaplain Mark worked with a middle school to address issues of bullying and dishonesty. He developed an ethical education program that included workshops, discussions, and role-playing exercises focused on empathy, respect, and honesty. He also facilitated conflict resolution sessions and provided ongoing support to students involved in bullying incidents. The program led to a noticeable decrease in bullying and an increase in positive behavior, creating a safer and more respectful school environment.

Fostering Community at a University:

At a university, Chaplain Sarah observed a lack of community among students from diverse backgrounds. She organized interfaith dialogues, cultural events, and community service projects to bring students together. She also provided support to international students, helping them adjust to campus life and feel included. These initiatives fostered a sense of belonging and mutual respect among students, enhancing the overall campus culture.

Navigating Crisis in a Primary School:

When a primary school faced the sudden loss of a beloved teacher, Chaplain James provided crucial support to the students, staff, and families. He led memorial services, offered grief counseling, and facilitated group discussions to help the school community process their emotions. His compassionate presence and support helped the school navigate the crisis and begin the healing process, reinforcing the importance of chaplaincy in times of loss and trauma.

Encouraging Civic Engagement in a College:

Chaplain Emily worked with a college to promote civic engagement among students. She organized voter registration drives, facilitated discussions on social justice issues, and led community service projects. She also mentored student leaders, helping them develop initiatives that addressed local needs. These efforts inspired a sense of civic responsibility and activism among students, leading to increased participation in community and political activities.

Challenges and Opportunities in Educational Chaplaincy

Addressing Diverse Needs: Educational settings are diverse, with students and staff from various cultural, religious, and socioeconomic backgrounds. Chaplains must be culturally competent and adaptable, providing inclusive support that respects and honors this diversity.

Balancing Roles: Chaplains often juggle multiple roles, including counselor, educator, mentor, and mediator. Balancing these responsibilities requires effective time management and the ability to prioritize the needs of the school community.

Resource Limitations: Limited resources, such as time and funding, can pose challenges to providing comprehensive chaplaincy services. Chaplains must advocate for the importance of their role and seek support from school leadership to effectively meet the needs of students and staff.

Leveraging Technology: Advances in technology offer new opportunities for chaplains to provide support. Virtual counseling sessions, online support groups, and digital resources can enhance the accessibility and reach of chaplaincy services.

Promoting Interfaith Understanding: Fostering interfaith understanding and respect is crucial in diverse educational settings. Chaplains play a key role in promoting dialogue and collaboration among students of different faith backgrounds, creating a more inclusive and harmonious school environment.

Educational chaplaincy is essential in fostering the spiritual, emotional, and ethical well-being of students, staff, and faculty in primary, secondary, and higher education settings. By providing pastoral care, promoting ethical behavior, fostering community, and supporting academic and personal growth, chaplains enhance the overall educational experience.

Supporting Students: Addressing the Spiritual, Emotional, and Ethical Needs of Students

Educational chaplaincy plays a critical role in supporting the holistic development of students. By addressing their spiritual, emotional, and ethical needs, chaplains help students navigate the challenges of academic life and personal growth. This chapter explores the various ways chaplains support students, highlighting the strategies they use and the impact of their work.

Understanding the Needs of Students

Spiritual Needs: Students often seek a sense of purpose, meaning, and connection in their lives. Spiritual support helps them explore and develop their beliefs, find inner peace, and build resilience.

Emotional Needs: The pressures of academic life, personal relationships, and future uncertainties can create significant emotional stress for students. Emotional support helps them manage stress, anxiety, and other mental health challenges.

Ethical Needs: As students develop their identities and make decisions that shape their futures, they encounter ethical dilemmas and challenges. Ethical support helps them navigate these situations with integrity and align their actions with their values.

Strategies for Supporting Students

Providing Spiritual Support:

1. Spiritual Counseling: Chaplains offer one-on-one spiritual counseling sessions where students can discuss their beliefs, explore their spirituality, and seek guidance. These sessions provide a safe space for students to express their concerns and find clarity.

2. Religious Services and Activities: Chaplains organize religious services, prayer groups, and spiritual activities that allow students to practice their faith and connect with others who share similar beliefs. These activities foster a sense of community and belonging.

3. Meditation and Mindfulness: Chaplains lead meditation and mindfulness sessions that help students cultivate inner peace and resilience. These practices support spiritual growth and provide tools for managing stress and anxiety.

Providing Emotional Support:

1. Counseling and Therapy: Chaplains provide counseling and therapeutic support to students dealing with a range of emotional issues, including stress, anxiety, depression, and relationship problems. They offer a compassionate and non-judgmental presence.

2. Support Groups: Chaplains facilitate support groups where students can share their experiences and offer mutual support. These groups create a sense of community and help students feel less isolated in their struggles.

3. Crisis Intervention: In times of crisis, such as the sudden loss of a loved one or a personal emergency, chaplains provide immediate and ongoing support. They help students process their emotions, offer practical assistance, and connect them with additional resources.

Providing Ethical Support:

1. Ethics Education: Chaplains conduct ethics education programs that teach students about moral values, ethical decision-making, and the importance of integrity. These programs help students develop a strong ethical foundation.

2. Conflict Resolution: Chaplains mediate conflicts between students, helping them resolve disputes peacefully and respectfully. They teach conflict resolution skills that students can apply in their personal and professional lives.

3. Role Modeling: Chaplains serve as role models for ethical behavior. Their actions and interactions demonstrate the importance of living with integrity, empathy, and respect, inspiring students to follow their example.

Case Studies in Supporting Students

Supporting Spiritual Growth in a High School:

At a high school, Chaplain Lisa noticed that many students were struggling with questions about their purpose and beliefs. She introduced a series of spiritual growth workshops that included discussions on faith, prayer, and meditation. She also offered individual spiritual counseling. These initiatives helped students explore their spirituality, find meaning in their lives, and develop resilience.

Providing Emotional Support in a Middle School:

Chaplain Mark worked with a middle school where students faced high levels of stress and anxiety, particularly during exam periods. He introduced stress management workshops, facilitated support groups, and provided individual counseling. As a result, students reported feeling more equipped to handle stress and better supported in their emotional well-being.

Promoting Ethical Behavior in a College:

At a college, Chaplain Sarah observed that students were facing ethical dilemmas related to academic integrity and personal conduct. She developed an ethics education program that included workshops, discussions, and case studies on ethical decision-making. She also provided confidential counseling to students dealing with specific ethical issues. The program led to a noticeable improvement in ethical behavior and a stronger culture of integrity on campus.

Crisis Intervention in a University:

When a university student experienced a personal tragedy, Chaplain James provided immediate crisis intervention. He offered grief counseling, facilitated support from the student's peers, and coordinated with university services to provide additional support. Chaplain James's compassionate presence and ongoing support helped the student navigate their grief and find the strength to continue their studies.

Encouraging Community Engagement in a Primary School:

At a primary school, Chaplain Emily noticed that students were disconnected from their community and lacked opportunities for social responsibility. She organized community service projects that involved students, teachers, and parents. These projects included clean-up drives, charity events, and visits to local nursing homes. The initiatives fostered a sense of social responsibility and community among the students, enhancing their personal growth and ethical development.

The Impact of Chaplaincy on Student Well-Being

Enhanced Spiritual Resilience: Students who receive spiritual support from chaplains develop a stronger sense of purpose and inner peace. This resilience helps them navigate academic and personal challenges with confidence and clarity.

Improved Emotional Health: Emotional support from chaplains leads to better mental health outcomes for students. They experience reduced stress, anxiety, and depression, and feel more supported in managing their emotional well-being.

Stronger Ethical Foundations: Ethical support helps students develop a solid foundation of values and principles. They become more adept at making ethical decisions and navigating moral dilemmas, contributing to their personal and professional growth.

Increased Academic Success: Students who receive holistic support from chaplains are better equipped to succeed academically. They manage stress more effectively, maintain a healthier work-life balance, and stay motivated and focused on their studies.

Fostering a Positive School Culture: Chaplains contribute to a positive and inclusive school culture by promoting respect, empathy, and community. Their efforts help create an environment where all students feel valued and supported.

Challenges and Opportunities in Supporting Students

Navigating Diverse Beliefs and Needs: Educational settings are diverse, with students from various cultural, religious, and socioeconomic backgrounds. Chaplains must be culturally competent and adaptable, providing inclusive support that respects and honors this diversity.

Balancing Roles and Responsibilities: Chaplains often juggle multiple roles, including counselor, educator, mentor, and mediator. Balancing these responsibilities requires effective time management and the ability to prioritize the needs of the school community.

Resource Limitations: Limited resources, such as time and funding, can pose challenges to providing comprehensive chaplaincy services. Chaplains must advocate for the importance of their role and seek support from school leadership to effectively meet the needs of students.

Leveraging Technology: Advances in technology offer new opportunities for chaplains to provide support. Virtual counseling sessions, online support groups, and digital resources can enhance the accessibility and reach of chaplaincy services.

Promoting Interfaith Understanding: Fostering interfaith understanding and respect is crucial in diverse educational settings. Chaplains play a key role in promoting dialogue and collaboration among students of different faith backgrounds, creating a more inclusive and harmonious school environment.

Educational chaplaincy is essential in supporting the spiritual, emotional, and ethical needs of students. By providing pastoral care, promoting ethical behavior, fostering community, and supporting academic and personal growth, chaplains enhance the overall educational experience.

Campus Ministries: The Development and Impact of Chaplaincy Programs in Universities

Campus ministries play a vital role in the life of universities, providing spiritual, emotional, and ethical support to students, faculty, and staff. These programs foster a sense of community, promote personal growth, and help individuals navigate the challenges of university life. This chapter explores the development and impact of chaplaincy programs in universities, highlighting their significance and the diverse ways they contribute to the academic environment.

The Development of Campus Ministries

Historical Background:

Campus ministries have a long history, dating back to the establishment of early universities where religious institutions played a central role in education. Initially, these programs were primarily focused on providing religious instruction and spiritual guidance to students.

Modern Evolution:

In modern times, campus ministries have evolved to address a broader range of spiritual, emotional, and ethical needs. They now encompass a wide variety of activities and services, from worship services and spiritual counseling to social justice initiatives and interfaith dialogue.

Institutional Support:

The development of campus ministries often involves collaboration between universities and religious organizations. Many universities have dedicated chaplaincy offices or centers that provide resources and support for these programs, ensuring they are integrated into the broader academic environment.

The Role of Campus Ministries

Providing Spiritual Support:

1. Worship Services: Campus ministries organize regular worship services that cater to different faith traditions.

These services provide students, faculty, and staff with opportunities for communal worship and spiritual renewal.

2. Spiritual Counseling: Chaplains offer one-on-one spiritual counseling, helping individuals explore their faith, seek guidance, and find comfort during difficult times. This support is crucial for students navigating the complexities of university life.

3. Religious Education: Campus ministries provide religious education through classes, study groups, and workshops. These programs help individuals deepen their understanding of their faith and engage with religious texts and traditions.

Fostering Emotional Well-Being:

1. Counseling Services: Chaplains offer emotional support and counseling to those dealing with stress, anxiety, depression, and other mental health issues. They provide a compassionate and non-judgmental presence, helping individuals manage their emotions and find healing.

2. Support Groups: Campus ministries facilitate support groups where students can share their experiences and offer mutual support. These groups create a sense of community and help individuals feel less isolated in their struggles.

3. Crisis Intervention: In times of crisis, such as personal loss or campus emergencies, chaplains provide immediate and ongoing support. They help individuals process their emotions, offer practical assistance, and coordinate with university services to provide comprehensive care.

Promoting Ethical and Moral Development:

1. Ethics Education: Campus ministries conduct ethics education programs that teach students about moral values, ethical decision-making, and social responsibility. These programs encourage students to develop strong ethical foundations and act with integrity.

2. Service Learning: Chaplains organize service learning projects that connect students with community service opportunities. These projects promote social responsibility and help students apply their ethical principles in real-world contexts.

3. Conflict Resolution: Chaplains mediate conflicts and help individuals resolve disputes peacefully and respectfully. They teach conflict resolution skills that students can use in their personal and professional lives.

Building Community and Inclusivity:

1. Interfaith Dialogue: Campus ministries promote interfaith dialogue and understanding, creating opportunities for individuals from different faith backgrounds to learn from

and support one another. These initiatives foster a more inclusive and respectful campus environment.

2. Community Events: Chaplains organize community events, such as cultural festivals, social gatherings, and workshops. These events bring together students, faculty, and staff, promoting a sense of belonging and community.

3. Support for Marginalized Groups: Campus ministries provide targeted support for marginalized and underrepresented groups. They advocate for inclusivity, offer specialized counseling, and create safe spaces for these individuals to share their experiences and find solidarity.

Case Studies in Campus Ministries

Fostering Interfaith Understanding at a Large University:

At a large university, Chaplain Laura developed an interfaith program that included dialogue sessions, collaborative service projects, and interfaith panels. These initiatives encouraged students from various religious backgrounds to share their beliefs and work together on community projects. The program fostered mutual respect and understanding, creating a more inclusive campus culture.

Supporting Mental Health at a Small Liberal Arts College:

Chaplain David at a small liberal arts college noticed increasing levels of anxiety and depression among students. He introduced mental health workshops, facilitated support groups, and offered individual counseling. His efforts provided students with the tools and support needed to manage their mental health, leading to improved well-being and academic performance.

Promoting Social Justice at an Urban University:

At an urban university, Chaplain Sarah organized social justice initiatives that engaged students in issues such as homelessness, food insecurity, and racial inequality. She led service learning projects, hosted educational events, and collaborated with local organizations. These initiatives raised awareness and inspired students to take action, contributing to positive change in the community.

Navigating Crisis at a Mid-Sized University:

When a tragic accident occurred on campus, Chaplain James provided critical support to the affected students, faculty, and staff. He organized memorial services, offered grief counseling, and facilitated community discussions. His compassionate presence helped the university community navigate the crisis and begin the healing process.

Encouraging Academic and Spiritual Growth at a Faith-Based College:

Chaplain Emily at a faith-based college integrated spiritual development into the academic experience. She offered religious education courses, organized retreats, and provided spiritual mentorship. Her efforts helped students grow both academically and spiritually, fostering a well-rounded and fulfilling college experience.

The Impact of Campus Ministries

Enhanced Spiritual and Emotional Well-Being: Campus ministries provide essential support that enhances the spiritual and emotional well-being of students, faculty, and staff. Individuals who engage with these programs report greater resilience, inner peace, and overall satisfaction with their university experience.

Stronger Ethical Foundations: Ethics education and service learning projects help students develop strong moral foundations. These experiences prepare them to act with integrity and social responsibility in their personal and professional lives.

Improved Academic Performance: Students who receive support from campus ministries often experience improved academic performance. The emotional and spiritual guidance they receive helps them manage stress, stay motivated, and maintain a healthy balance between their studies and personal lives.

Fostering a Positive Campus Culture: Campus ministries contribute to a positive and inclusive campus culture by promoting respect, empathy, and community. Their efforts create an environment where all individuals feel valued and supported.

Increased Community Engagement: Service learning and social justice initiatives inspire students to engage with their communities and make a positive impact. These experiences foster a sense of civic responsibility and empower students to contribute to the greater good.

Challenges and Opportunities in Campus Ministries

Addressing Diverse Needs: Universities are diverse environments with students from various cultural, religious, and socioeconomic backgrounds. Chaplains must be culturally competent and adaptable, providing inclusive support that respects and honors this diversity.

Balancing Roles and Responsibilities: Chaplains often juggle multiple roles, including counselor, educator, mentor, and mediator. Balancing these responsibilities requires effective time management and the ability to prioritize the needs of the university community.

Resource Limitations: Limited resources, such as time and funding, can pose challenges to providing comprehensive chaplaincy services. Chaplains must advocate for the importance of their role and seek support from university leadership to effectively meet the needs of students, faculty, and staff.

Leveraging Technology: Advances in technology offer new opportunities for chaplains to provide support. Virtual counseling sessions, online support groups, and digital resources can enhance the accessibility and reach of chaplaincy services.

Promoting Interfaith Understanding: Fostering interfaith understanding and respect is crucial in diverse university settings. Chaplains play a key role in promoting dialogue and collaboration among individuals of different faith backgrounds, creating a more inclusive and harmonious campus environment.

Campus ministries are essential in fostering the spiritual, emotional, and ethical well-being of students, faculty, and staff in universities. By providing pastoral care, promoting ethical behavior, fostering community, and supporting academic and personal growth, chaplains enhance the overall educational experience.

Narratives: Personal Stories of Chaplains Making a Difference in Educational Settings

The impact of chaplaincy in educational settings can be deeply personal and transformative. This chapter presents narratives that highlight the ways in which chaplains make a significant difference in the lives of students, faculty, and staff. These stories provide insight into the diverse roles chaplains play and the profound effects of their work.

Narrative 1: Finding Faith and Purpose

Context: High School

Chaplain: Chaplain Laura

Story:

Sophomore year was a challenging time for Emily, a high school student struggling with questions about her faith and purpose in life. She felt disconnected from her peers and unsure about her future. Chaplain Laura noticed Emily's struggles and invited her to join a small group discussion on faith and spirituality.

Through these weekly meetings, Emily found a safe space to express her doubts and explore her beliefs. Chaplain Laura provided guidance and support, helping Emily see the value of her unique journey. Over time, Emily began to find clarity and purpose, becoming more engaged in school activities and building stronger relationships with her classmates.

Emily's transformation was evident to her teachers and peers. She attributed much of her newfound confidence and direction to the support she received from Chaplain Laura. This narrative illustrates the profound impact of spiritual guidance on a student's personal growth and development.

Narrative 2: Overcoming Grief and Loss

Context: Middle School

Chaplain: Chaplain David

Story:

When Michael, a seventh-grader, lost his mother to cancer, his world was turned upside down. He became withdrawn, his grades suffered, and he had difficulty connecting with his friends. Chaplain David reached out to Michael, offering a compassionate ear and a shoulder to lean on.

Through regular counseling sessions, Chaplain David helped Michael navigate his grief. He also introduced Michael to a support group for students who had experienced loss. In this group, Michael found others who understood his pain, and he began to open up about his feelings.

With Chaplain David's support, Michael gradually started to heal. He found ways to honor his mother's memory and cope with his emotions. His academic performance improved, and he reconnected with his friends. Michael's story is a testament to the critical role of chaplains in helping students through the darkest times of their lives.

Narrative 3: Promoting Ethical Leadership

Context: College

Chaplain: Chaplain Sarah

Story:

Jacob, a college junior, was elected president of the student government. Although excited about the opportunity, he quickly faced ethical dilemmas and leadership challenges. He struggled with balancing his responsibilities and maintaining his integrity.

Chaplain Sarah noticed Jacob's difficulties and offered her support. She provided him with ethical guidance, helping him navigate complex situations and make decisions that aligned with his values. Chaplain Sarah also mentored Jacob, teaching him leadership skills and the importance of empathy and integrity.

Under Chaplain Sarah's mentorship, Jacob flourished as a leader. He became more confident in his role and gained the respect of his peers. He led the student government with a strong ethical foundation, making decisions that benefited the entire student body. Jacob's experience highlights the role of chaplains in cultivating ethical leadership in educational settings.

Narrative 4: Building Community and Inclusivity

Context: University

Chaplain: Chaplain James

Story:

At a diverse university, tensions between different cultural and religious groups occasionally flared up, creating a fragmented campus environment. Chaplain James saw an opportunity to bridge these divides and foster a sense of unity.

He organized a series of interfaith dialogues and cultural exchange events. These gatherings provided a platform for students to share their beliefs and traditions, fostering mutual respect and understanding. Chaplain James also facilitated collaborative service projects, bringing students together to work towards common goals.

Through these initiatives, the campus culture began to shift. Students developed deeper connections with one another, and the atmosphere became more inclusive and supportive. Chaplain James's efforts demonstrated the power of chaplaincy in building community and promoting inclusivity in a diverse educational setting.

Narrative 5: Supporting Mental Health

Context: High School

Chaplain: Chaplain Emily

Story:

Samantha, a high school senior, was struggling with severe anxiety and depression. The pressure of upcoming exams and college applications exacerbated her mental health issues. Her teachers were concerned but unsure how to help.

Chaplain Emily stepped in, offering Samantha regular counseling sessions. She provided a safe space for Samantha to express her fears and anxieties. Chaplain Emily also taught her mindfulness techniques and stress management strategies, which Samantha found immensely helpful.

With Chaplain Emily's ongoing support, Samantha's mental health began to improve. She felt more equipped to handle her stress and became more engaged in her studies and social life. Samantha successfully graduated and was accepted into her first-choice college. Her story underscores the essential role of chaplains in supporting students' mental health and well-being.

Narrative 6: Encouraging Academic and Personal Growth

Context: University

Chaplain: Chaplain Mark

Story:

Alex, a university sophomore, was struggling academically and personally. He felt overwhelmed by the demands of his coursework and uncertain about his future. He frequently skipped classes and considered dropping out.

Chaplain Mark noticed Alex's distress and reached out to offer support. Through regular meetings, Chaplain Mark helped Alex develop a study plan and set realistic goals. He also provided emotional support, helping Alex build confidence and resilience.

Under Chaplain Mark's guidance, Alex began to turn things around. His grades improved, and he regained his motivation and focus. Alex also became involved in campus activities, building a network of supportive friends. This narrative highlights the transformative impact of chaplaincy on a student's academic and personal growth.

These narratives demonstrate the profound and diverse impact of chaplains in educational settings. By addressing the spiritual, emotional, and ethical needs of students, chaplains play a crucial role in fostering personal growth, community, and well-being. Their compassionate presence and support make a significant difference in the lives of students, faculty, and staff, underscoring the essential role of chaplaincy in education.

CHAPTER 07

CORRECTIONAL CHAPLAINCY

History and Development: The Evolution of Chaplaincy in Correctional Facilities

Correctional chaplaincy has played a significant role in the rehabilitation and support of incarcerated individuals. The evolution of chaplaincy in correctional facilities reflects broader changes in the criminal justice system, societal attitudes towards punishment and rehabilitation, and the recognition of the importance of spiritual care. This chapter explores the history and development of correctional chaplaincy, highlighting its key milestones and impact on the correctional environment.

Early Beginnings

Origins in Religious Care:

The concept of providing spiritual care to prisoners dates back to ancient times. Religious leaders often visited prisoners to offer comfort, counsel, and religious rites. In medieval Europe, monasteries sometimes served as places of confinement, where monks would provide spiritual guidance to those detained.

Colonial Era:

In the colonial era, chaplaincy began to take a more organized form in correctional facilities. Chaplains, often associated with specific religious denominations, were appointed to minister to the spiritual needs of prisoners. Their roles included conducting worship services, offering religious education, and providing moral guidance.

The 19th Century: Institutionalization and Reform

Prison Reform Movements:

The 19th century saw significant prison reform movements, particularly in the United States and Europe. Reformers like John Howard and Elizabeth Fry advocated for the humane treatment of prisoners and the importance of rehabilitation over mere punishment. These movements emphasized the need for moral and spiritual reform, leading to a more structured role for chaplains in correctional facilities.

Formal Chaplaincy Roles:

During this period, formal chaplaincy roles were established in many prisons. Chaplains were employed by the state or religious organizations to provide regular spiritual services, counseling, and support to inmates. Their work was seen as essential to the moral and spiritual rehabilitation of prisoners.

Expansion of Services:

Chaplains began to expand their services beyond religious instruction and worship. They offered educational programs, vocational training, and personal counseling, recognizing the need for a holistic approach to rehabilitation. This period marked the beginning of a more comprehensive model of correctional chaplaincy.

The 20th Century: Professionalization and Diversification

Professionalization of Chaplaincy:

The 20th century brought significant professionalization to the field of chaplaincy. Correctional chaplains received specialized training in theology, counseling, and correctional practices. Professional associations and accrediting bodies were established to ensure high standards and accountability.

Interfaith Chaplaincy:

As societies became more religiously diverse, correctional chaplaincy adapted to meet the needs of inmates from various faith traditions. Interfaith chaplaincy programs were developed to provide inclusive spiritual care, ensuring that all prisoners had access to religious support and resources.

Integration with Rehabilitation Programs:

Chaplains increasingly integrated their work with broader rehabilitation programs within correctional facilities. They collaborated with psychologists, social workers, and educators to address the spiritual, emotional, and practical needs of inmates. This interdisciplinary approach enhanced the effectiveness of rehabilitation efforts.

The Modern Era: Challenges and Innovations

Human Rights and Spiritual Care:

In the modern era, there is a growing recognition of the importance of spiritual care as a fundamental human right for prisoners. International standards and guidelines, such as those from the United Nations, emphasize the need for access to religious services and support in correctional facilities.

Innovative Programs:

Correctional chaplaincy has seen numerous innovative programs designed to support inmate rehabilitation and reentry into society. These programs include restorative justice initiatives, faith-based educational courses, and support groups for specific populations, such as veterans and women.

Use of Technology:

Advances in technology have also impacted correctional chaplaincy. Chaplains now use digital platforms to provide religious education, counseling, and worship services. This is particularly important in large facilities or during times of restricted access, such as during the COVID-19 pandemic.

Impact of Correctional Chaplaincy

Spiritual and Emotional Support:

Correctional chaplains provide essential spiritual and emotional support to inmates, helping them cope with the challenges of incarceration. Through counseling, religious services, and personal interactions, chaplains offer hope, comfort, and guidance.

Moral and Ethical Guidance:

Chaplains play a crucial role in the moral and ethical development of inmates. They encourage self-reflection, accountability, and positive change, fostering a sense of responsibility and moral integrity.

Rehabilitation and Reentry:

Chaplains contribute significantly to the rehabilitation and reentry of inmates. By addressing spiritual needs and promoting personal growth, chaplains help inmates develop the skills and mindset necessary for successful reintegration into society.

Reduction of Recidivism:

Studies have shown that inmates who participate in chaplaincy programs and receive spiritual care are less likely to reoffend. The positive influence of chaplains helps reduce recidivism rates, contributing to safer communities and more effective correctional systems.

Case Studies in Correctional Chaplaincy

Restorative Justice Programs:

In a state prison, Chaplain Michael implemented a restorative justice program that brought together victims and offenders for facilitated dialogues. This program aimed to promote healing, accountability, and reconciliation. The initiative received positive feedback from both victims and inmates, highlighting the transformative potential of restorative justice.

Faith-Based Educational Courses:

Chaplain Maria at a federal correctional facility developed a series of faith-based educational courses that included Bible study, ethical decision-making, and vocational training. These courses provided inmates with valuable skills and moral guidance, helping them prepare for life after release.

Support for Veterans:

Recognizing the unique needs of incarcerated veterans, Chaplain John established a support group specifically for this population. The group provided a space for veterans to share their experiences, receive spiritual support, and access resources tailored to their needs. This initiative significantly improved the well-being and rehabilitation outcomes for veteran inmates.

Reentry Support Programs:

Chaplain Lisa worked with a local jail to create a reentry support program that included pre-release counseling, connection to community resources, and ongoing spiritual support after release. This program helped inmates transition back into society more smoothly, reducing the likelihood of reoffending.

Challenges and Opportunities in Correctional Chaplaincy

Addressing Diverse Needs:

Correctional facilities house individuals from diverse cultural, religious, and socioeconomic backgrounds. Chaplains must be culturally competent and adaptable, providing inclusive support that respects and honors this diversity.

Balancing Roles and Responsibilities:

Chaplains often juggle multiple roles, including counselor, educator, mediator, and advocate. Balancing these responsibilities requires effective time management and the ability to prioritize the needs of inmates and staff.

Resource Limitations:

Limited resources, such as time, funding, and access to facilities, can pose challenges to providing comprehensive chaplaincy services. Chaplains must advocate for the importance of their role and seek support from correctional leadership to effectively meet the needs of inmates.

Promoting Interfaith Understanding:

Fostering interfaith understanding and respect is crucial in correctional settings. Chaplains play a key role in promoting dialogue and collaboration among inmates of different faith backgrounds, creating a more inclusive and harmonious environment.

Correctional chaplaincy has evolved significantly over the centuries, from its early beginnings to the modern, professionalized, and diverse field it is today. Chaplains provide essential spiritual, emotional, and ethical support to incarcerated individuals, playing a crucial role in their rehabilitation and reentry into society.

Rehabilitation and Reform: How Chaplains Contribute to the Rehabilitation and Spiritual Growth of Inmates

The role of chaplains in correctional facilities extends far beyond providing religious services. They are integral to the rehabilitation and spiritual growth of inmates, offering support, guidance, and programs designed to foster personal transformation. This chapter explores the ways in which chaplains contribute to the rehabilitation and reform of inmates, highlighting their unique approaches and the impact of their work.

The Role of Chaplains in Rehabilitation

Providing Emotional and Spiritual Support:

1. Counseling Services: Chaplains offer one-on-one counseling to inmates, helping them process emotions, deal with trauma, and navigate the challenges of incarceration. This support is crucial for inmates' mental health and emotional stability.

2. Spiritual Guidance: Chaplains provide spiritual guidance, helping inmates explore their faith, find meaning and purpose, and develop a sense of hope. This spiritual

support is a key component of inmates' overall well-being and personal growth.

3. Crisis Intervention: In times of crisis, such as the death of a loved one or personal trauma, chaplains provide immediate and ongoing support. They help inmates cope with grief, loss, and other intense emotions, offering a compassionate presence and practical assistance.

Facilitating Personal Transformation:

1. Religious Services: Chaplains conduct regular religious services, including worship, prayer, and religious education. These services provide a sense of community and belonging, fostering spiritual growth and personal reflection.

2. Faith-Based Programs: Chaplains develop and facilitate faith-based programs that address various aspects of personal development, such as anger management, forgiveness, and ethical decision-making. These programs help inmates develop positive attitudes and behaviors.

3. Restorative Justice: Chaplains often lead restorative justice programs that promote accountability, reconciliation, and healing. These programs involve dialogues between victims and offenders, aiming to repair harm and rebuild trust.

Promoting Ethical and Moral Development:

1. Ethics Education: Chaplains provide ethics education, teaching inmates about moral values, ethical

decision-making, and the importance of integrity. This education helps inmates develop a strong ethical foundation.

2. Role Modeling: Chaplains serve as role models for ethical behavior. Their actions and interactions demonstrate the importance of living with integrity, empathy, and respect, inspiring inmates to follow their example.

3. Conflict Resolution: Chaplains mediate conflicts within the inmate population, promoting peaceful and respectful resolution of disputes. They teach conflict resolution skills that inmates can use both during and after incarceration.

Programs and Initiatives for Rehabilitation

Educational and Vocational Training:

1. Educational Programs: Chaplains often collaborate with educational providers to offer literacy classes, GED preparation, and higher education opportunities. These programs equip inmates with valuable skills and knowledge that enhance their prospects for reintegration.

2. Vocational Training: Chaplains support vocational training programs that teach inmates practical skills in trades such as carpentry, plumbing, and culinary arts. These programs increase inmates' employability and self-sufficiency upon release.

3. Life Skills Training: Chaplains facilitate life skills training, covering areas such as financial literacy, time

management, and parenting. These skills are essential for inmates' successful reentry into society.

Support Groups and Peer Mentoring:

1. Support Groups: Chaplains organize support groups for various issues, including addiction recovery, anger management, and grief. These groups provide a supportive environment where inmates can share experiences and support each other.

2. Peer Mentoring: Chaplains train inmates to become peer mentors, offering guidance and support to fellow inmates. Peer mentoring programs foster a sense of responsibility and leadership, contributing to a positive prison culture.

3. Faith-Based Support Groups: Chaplains lead faith-based support groups that combine spiritual guidance with practical support. These groups help inmates integrate their faith into their daily lives and personal growth.

Reentry and Reintegration Programs:

1. Reentry Planning: Chaplains assist inmates in developing reentry plans that address housing, employment, and community support. They provide resources and connections to community organizations that support reentry.

2. Family Reunification: Chaplains facilitate family reunification programs that help inmates rebuild relationships with their families. These programs include counseling, communication skills training, and family visits.

3. Aftercare Support: Chaplains provide ongoing support to inmates after their release, helping them navigate the challenges of reentry. This support includes spiritual counseling, mentoring, and connections to community resources.

Impact of Chaplaincy on Rehabilitation and Reform

Spiritual Growth and Transformation:

1. Personal Reflection: Chaplaincy programs encourage inmates to engage in personal reflection and self-examination. This process helps inmates understand the impact of their actions and develop a desire for positive change.

2. Sense of Purpose: Through spiritual guidance and religious activities, chaplains help inmates find a sense of purpose and meaning in their lives. This sense of purpose is a powerful motivator for personal growth and rehabilitation.

3. Healing and Forgiveness: Chaplains support inmates in the process of healing and forgiveness, both for themselves and others. This emotional and spiritual healing is essential for inmates' overall well-being and transformation.

Reduction of Recidivism:

1. Positive Behavior Changes: Chaplaincy programs promote positive behavior changes, reducing disciplinary infractions and promoting a safer prison environment. Inmates who participate in these programs are more likely to adopt constructive attitudes and behaviors.

2. Improved Reentry Outcomes: Inmates who receive chaplaincy support are better prepared for reentry into society. They have higher rates of employment, stable housing, and positive social connections, reducing the likelihood of reoffending.

3. Long-Term Success: Chaplaincy programs contribute to the long-term success of inmates by fostering personal growth, spiritual resilience, and ethical development. These programs help inmates build a foundation for a productive and fulfilling life after incarceration.

Case Studies in Chaplaincy and Rehabilitation

Faith-Based Educational Programs:

Chaplain Maria at a federal correctional facility developed a faith-based educational program that included Bible study, ethical decision-making, and vocational training. These courses provided inmates with valuable skills and moral guidance, helping them prepare for life after release. The program received positive feedback from participants and contributed to lower recidivism rates.

Restorative Justice Initiatives:

In a state prison, Chaplain Michael implemented a restorative justice program that brought together victims and offenders for facilitated dialogues. This program aimed to promote healing, accountability, and reconciliation. The initiative received positive feedback from both victims and inmates, highlighting the transformative potential of restorative justice.

Support Groups for Addiction Recovery:

Chaplain Lisa at a local jail established support groups for inmates struggling with addiction. These groups combined spiritual guidance with practical recovery strategies, providing a comprehensive approach to addiction recovery. Many participants reported significant progress in their recovery journeys, crediting the support and guidance of the chaplaincy program.

Reentry Support Programs:

Chaplain John worked with a state prison to create a reentry support program that included pre-release counseling, connection to community resources, and ongoing spiritual support after release. This program helped inmates transition back into society more smoothly, reducing the likelihood of reoffending. The success of the program led to its expansion to other facilities in the state.

Challenges and Opportunities in Rehabilitation and Reform

Addressing Diverse Needs:

Correctional facilities house individuals from diverse cultural, religious, and socioeconomic backgrounds. Chaplains must be culturally competent and adaptable, providing inclusive support that respects and honors this diversity.

Balancing Roles and Responsibilities:

Chaplains often juggle multiple roles, including counselor, educator, mediator, and advocate. Balancing these responsibilities requires effective time management and the ability to prioritize the needs of inmates.

Resource Limitations:

Limited resources, such as time, funding, and access to facilities, can pose challenges to providing comprehensive chaplaincy services. Chaplains must advocate for the importance of their role and seek support from correctional leadership to effectively meet the needs of inmates.

Promoting Interfaith Understanding:

Fostering interfaith understanding and respect is crucial in correctional settings. Chaplains play a key role in promoting dialogue and collaboration among inmates of different faith backgrounds, creating a more inclusive and harmonious environment.

Leveraging Technology:

Advances in technology offer new opportunities for chaplains to provide support. Virtual counseling sessions, online support groups, and digital resources can enhance the accessibility and reach of chaplaincy services.

Chaplains are indispensable to the rehabilitation and spiritual growth of inmates. Through counseling, spiritual guidance, educational programs, and reentry support, chaplains foster personal transformation, ethical development, and successful reintegration into society. Their work significantly contributes to reducing recidivism and promoting safer, more constructive correctional environments.

Ethical Considerations: The Unique Ethical Challenges Faced by Correctional Chaplains

Correctional chaplaincy is a field fraught with unique ethical challenges. Chaplains working in correctional facilities must navigate complex situations involving the welfare of inmates, their own professional integrity, and the operational constraints of the institutions they serve. This chapter explores the various ethical considerations that correctional chaplains face, highlighting the dilemmas, responsibilities, and strategies for ethical decision-making.

Understanding Ethical Challenges in Correctional Chaplaincy

Dual Loyalties: Correctional chaplains often find themselves balancing dual loyalties—to the inmates they serve and the correctional system that employs them. This can create conflicts, especially when the needs of inmates and the policies of the institution are at odds.

Confidentiality and Trust: Maintaining confidentiality is a cornerstone of chaplaincy. However, in a correctional setting, there are limits to confidentiality, particularly when it comes to security concerns or mandatory reporting obligations. Chaplains must navigate these boundaries carefully to maintain trust while adhering to legal and institutional requirements.

Power Dynamics: The inherent power dynamics within correctional facilities can impact the chaplain-inmate relationship. Chaplains must be aware of these dynamics and strive to create an environment of mutual respect and support, without compromising their professional boundaries.

Cultural and Religious Diversity: Correctional facilities house individuals from diverse cultural and religious backgrounds. Chaplains must provide inclusive and respectful support, regardless of their own religious beliefs or cultural backgrounds. This requires sensitivity, cultural competence, and a commitment to interfaith respect.

Key Ethical Challenges and Considerations

Maintaining Confidentiality:

1. Balancing Confidentiality and Security: Chaplains must protect the confidentiality of inmates while also adhering to institutional policies that require reporting certain information for security reasons. This balance is delicate and requires clear communication with inmates about the limits of confidentiality.

2. Mandatory Reporting: Chaplains are often required to report instances of harm or threats to safety. They must navigate the tension between maintaining trust with inmates and fulfilling their legal and ethical obligations to report.

3. Building Trust: Establishing and maintaining trust is crucial in correctional chaplaincy. Chaplains must be transparent about the boundaries of confidentiality and consistently demonstrate integrity in their interactions with inmates.

Navigating Dual Loyalties:

1. Inmate Advocacy: Chaplains serve as advocates for the spiritual and emotional well-being of inmates. This role can sometimes conflict with institutional policies or practices. Chaplains must find ways to advocate effectively within the constraints of the correctional system.

2. Institutional Loyalty: As employees of the correctional system, chaplains have a responsibility to support the institution's mission and policies. Balancing this loyalty with their commitment to inmate care requires careful ethical consideration and negotiation.

3. Conflict Resolution: When conflicts arise between the needs of inmates and institutional policies, chaplains must employ conflict resolution skills to navigate these challenges. This may involve mediating between inmates and staff or seeking creative solutions that honor both parties' needs.

Managing Power Dynamics:

1. Professional Boundaries: Chaplains must maintain professional boundaries to ensure the integrity of the chaplain-inmate relationship. This includes avoiding dual relationships, maintaining appropriate distance, and not using their position for personal gain.

2. Empowerment: Chaplains should strive to empower inmates, fostering a sense of agency and self-worth.

This involves providing resources, support, and opportunities for personal growth while respecting inmates' autonomy.

3. Mutual Respect: Establishing mutual respect is essential for effective chaplaincy. Chaplains must treat inmates with dignity and respect, recognizing their inherent worth as individuals, regardless of their past actions.

Cultural and Religious Sensitivity:

1. Inclusive Support: Chaplains must provide support that is inclusive of all cultural and religious backgrounds. This requires an understanding of different traditions and a willingness to accommodate diverse spiritual needs.

2. Interfaith Collaboration: Promoting interfaith understanding and respect is a key component of correctional chaplaincy. Chaplains should facilitate interfaith dialogue, collaborate with religious leaders from different faiths, and create opportunities for inmates to explore their spirituality in a supportive environment.

3. Cultural Competence: Chaplains must continually develop their cultural competence, seeking to understand and respect the diverse backgrounds of the inmates they serve. This includes ongoing education, self-reflection, and a commitment to challenging personal biases.

Strategies for Ethical Decision-Making

Ethical Reflection and Self-Awareness:

1. Regular Reflection: Chaplains should engage in regular ethical reflection to examine their actions, decisions, and motivations. This practice helps maintain ethical integrity and fosters personal growth.

2. Supervision and Peer Support: Seeking supervision and peer support provides chaplains with opportunities to discuss ethical dilemmas, receive feedback, and gain new perspectives. This collaborative approach enhances ethical decision-making.

3. Self-Awareness: Developing self-awareness is crucial for ethical chaplaincy. Chaplains must be aware of their own biases, limitations, and emotional responses, and strive to act with humility and integrity.

Education and Training:

1. Continuous Learning: Chaplains should pursue ongoing education and training in ethics, cultural competence, and professional standards. This commitment to lifelong learning ensures they are equipped to navigate complex ethical challenges.

2. Workshops and Seminars: Participating in workshops and seminars on ethical issues in chaplaincy provides opportunities for learning and professional development. These events facilitate knowledge sharing and the exploration of best practices.

3. Ethics Committees: Involving chaplains in institutional ethics committees allows them to contribute their expertise to broader ethical discussions and decisions within the correctional facility.

Ethical Guidelines and Frameworks:

1. Code of Ethics: Adhering to a code of ethics provides a foundational framework for ethical decision-making. Chaplains should be familiar with the ethical guidelines of their profession and strive to uphold these standards.

2. Ethical Frameworks: Utilizing ethical frameworks, such as the principles of beneficence, non-maleficence, autonomy, and justice, helps chaplains navigate complex situations and make balanced decisions.

3. Institutional Policies: Understanding and adhering to institutional policies is essential for ethical chaplaincy. Chaplains should be aware of the policies that govern their work and advocate for changes when these policies conflict with ethical principles.

Case Studies in Ethical Decision-Making

Balancing Confidentiality and Security:

Chaplain Michael encountered a situation where an inmate disclosed plans to harm another inmate. Michael faced the ethical dilemma of maintaining confidentiality versus the need to report the threat for safety reasons. He chose to report the threat, explaining the limits of confidentiality to the inmate. Michael's decision protected the safety of the inmate population while maintaining transparency about his ethical responsibilities.

Navigating Dual Loyalties:

Chaplain Maria was approached by an inmate who felt unjustly treated by the correctional staff. Maria listened to the inmate's concerns and advocated for a fair review of the situation, while also maintaining her professional relationship with the staff. By facilitating a constructive dialogue, Maria helped address the inmate's grievances and promoted a more just and respectful institutional environment.

Managing Power Dynamics:

Chaplain John noticed that an inmate was becoming overly dependent on him for emotional support. Recognizing the need to maintain professional boundaries, John referred the inmate to additional support services within the facility and encouraged peer mentoring. This approach empowered the inmate while ensuring that John's professional boundaries remained intact.

Promoting Interfaith Respect:

Chaplain Lisa worked in a facility with a diverse inmate population. She organized interfaith events that allowed inmates to share their religious practices and beliefs. When conflicts arose between inmates of different faiths, Lisa facilitated respectful dialogues that promoted understanding and mutual respect. Her efforts fostered a more inclusive and harmonious environment.

Challenges and Opportunities in Ethical Chaplaincy

Resource Limitations: Limited resources can pose significant challenges to ethical chaplaincy. Chaplains must advocate for adequate support and find creative ways to maximize the impact of their services.

Institutional Constraints: Chaplains often operate within strict institutional constraints. Navigating these constraints while upholding ethical principles requires skill, diplomacy, and persistence.

Continuous Development: Ethical chaplaincy requires ongoing development and self-improvement. Chaplains must remain committed to their own professional growth, seeking opportunities to enhance their skills and knowledge.

Advocacy and Change: Chaplains have the opportunity to advocate for ethical practices and reforms within correctional facilities. By promoting justice, respect, and human dignity, chaplains can contribute to positive changes in the correctional system.

Ethical considerations are central to the practice of correctional chaplaincy. Chaplains face unique ethical challenges that require careful reflection, integrity, and a commitment to the well-being of the inmates they serve. By maintaining confidentiality, navigating dual loyalties, managing power dynamics, and promoting cultural and religious sensitivity, chaplains uphold the highest standards of ethical practice.

Transformative Stories: Accounts of Lives Changed Through the Work of Correctional Chaplains

Correctional chaplains play a crucial role in the rehabilitation and spiritual growth of inmates. Their work often leads to profound transformations, helping individuals find hope, meaning, and a new direction in life. This chapter presents a series of transformative stories, highlighting the significant impact of chaplains on the lives of those they serve within correctional facilities.

Story 1: Finding Redemption Through Faith

Inmate: Robert

Chaplain: Chaplain Maria

Story:

Robert was serving a lengthy sentence for a series of violent crimes. He was filled with anger, bitterness, and regret, struggling to find a sense of purpose. Chaplain Maria met Robert during one of her regular visits to the prison. She offered him a listening ear and introduced him to spiritual practices that could help him find peace.

Over time, Robert began attending Bible study sessions and participating in group prayers led by Chaplain Maria. He found solace in the teachings and began to reflect deeply on his past actions. Through their conversations, Robert started to see a path toward redemption. He embraced his faith and committed himself to personal transformation.

Robert's behavior changed dramatically. He became a mentor to younger inmates, sharing his story and encouraging them to seek positive change. Upon his release, Robert continued his spiritual journey, becoming an active member of his church and community. His transformation is a testament to the power of faith and the guidance of a dedicated chaplain.

Story 2: Overcoming Addiction and Rebuilding Life

Inmate: Lisa

Chaplain: Chaplain John

Story:

Lisa was incarcerated due to her involvement in drug-related offenses. She had struggled with addiction for many years, which had led her down a path of crime and self-destruction. Chaplain John first met Lisa during an addiction recovery program he facilitated at the prison.

Chaplain John provided Lisa with spiritual counseling and support, helping her understand the underlying issues contributing to her addiction. He introduced her to a faith-based recovery group that met regularly to discuss challenges, share experiences, and offer mutual support.

With Chaplain John's guidance, Lisa began to rebuild her life. She found strength in her faith and the support of her recovery group. She completed vocational training and earned her GED while in prison, preparing for a new start after her release.

Upon leaving prison, Lisa continued to receive support from Chaplain John and her recovery community. She secured a job, maintained her sobriety, and reconnected with her family. Lisa's story demonstrates the transformative impact of chaplaincy on individuals battling addiction.

Story 3: Healing and Forgiveness Through Restorative Justice

Inmate: Mark

Chaplain: Chaplain Emily

Story:

Mark was serving a sentence for a serious assault that had left the victim with lasting injuries. He was consumed by guilt and unable to forgive himself for his actions. Chaplain Emily introduced Mark to a restorative justice program that aimed to facilitate healing and reconciliation between offenders and their victims.

With Chaplain Emily's support, Mark participated in mediated dialogues with his victim. These sessions were emotionally intense, but they allowed both parties to express their feelings, ask questions, and seek understanding. Mark had the opportunity to apologize and take responsibility for his actions.

The restorative justice process was transformative for Mark. He experienced a profound sense of healing and forgiveness, both from his victim and himself. He began to volunteer for various programs within the prison, helping others on their path to rehabilitation.

Mark's story highlights the power of restorative justice and the crucial role of chaplains in facilitating these life-changing processes. Through Chaplain Emily's guidance, Mark found a way to make amends and turn his life around.

Story 4: Reconnecting with Family and Building a New Future

Inmate: James

Chaplain: Chaplain David

Story:

James was estranged from his family due to his criminal activities and incarceration. He felt isolated and hopeless, doubting that he could ever rebuild those broken relationships. Chaplain David took a special interest in James's situation and began working with him on family reconciliation.

Chaplain David facilitated communication between James and his family, encouraging them to write letters and eventually arranging visits. He provided counseling to help James address the issues that had led to the estrangement and to prepare him for rebuilding trust with his loved ones.

Through these efforts, James gradually reconnected with his family. His parents and siblings visited him regularly, and they started to rebuild their relationships. James's renewed sense of purpose and hope was evident in his behavior and outlook on life.

After his release, James moved back home and continued to work on his relationship with his family. He found a job and became involved in community service, inspired by Chaplain David's dedication and support. James's story illustrates the importance of family reconciliation in the rehabilitation process and the pivotal role of chaplains in facilitating these reunions.

Story 5: Embracing Education and Personal Growth

Inmate: Sarah

Chaplain: Chaplain Lisa

Story:

Sarah was a young woman who had dropped out of school and turned to a life of crime. She lacked direction and self-worth, feeling that her future was bleak. Chaplain Lisa met Sarah during an educational program she offered at the prison, focusing on personal development and spiritual growth.

Chaplain Lisa encouraged Sarah to continue her education and provided her with the resources and support she needed to do so. Sarah enrolled in the GED program and began attending classes regularly. Chaplain Lisa also offered spiritual counseling, helping Sarah explore her faith and find inner strength.

Sarah's dedication paid off, and she earned her GED. Motivated by this achievement, she pursued further education through correspondence courses offered by a local community college. Chaplain Lisa's unwavering support and encouragement were instrumental in Sarah's journey.

Upon her release, Sarah continued her education and eventually earned an associate degree. She found employment in a field she was passionate about and became an advocate for education and rehabilitation programs for formerly incarcerated individuals. Sarah's transformation underscores the transformative power of education and the essential role of chaplains in inspiring and supporting personal growth.

These transformative stories highlight the profound impact of correctional chaplains on the lives of inmates. Through their dedication, compassion, and spiritual guidance, chaplains help individuals find hope, healing, and a path to a better future. Their work fosters personal transformation, rehabilitation, and reintegration, demonstrating the essential role of chaplaincy in correctional facilities.

CHAPTER 08

THE ETHICAL FRAMEWORK OF CHPALINCY

Confidentiality and Trust: Maintaining Confidentiality and Building Trust with Those Served

Confidentiality and trust are fundamental elements of chaplaincy, forming the bedrock upon which effective spiritual care and support are built. In the context of correctional chaplaincy, these principles are particularly critical due to the unique environment and the vulnerabilities of the inmate population. This chapter delves into the ethical importance of confidentiality and trust, the challenges chaplains face in maintaining these principles, and strategies for effectively building and preserving trust with those they serve.

The Ethical Importance of Confidentiality

Defining Confidentiality:

Confidentiality in chaplaincy refers to the obligation to keep private the information shared by those seeking spiritual care. This includes personal, emotional, and spiritual disclosures made in the context of counseling or pastoral care.

The Role of Confidentiality in Chaplaincy:

1. Building Trust: Confidentiality is essential for building trust between chaplains and those they serve. When individuals know that their disclosures will be kept private, they are more likely to open up and seek help.

2. Providing Safe Spaces: Confidentiality creates a safe space for individuals to express their deepest fears, doubts, and hopes without fear of judgment or reprisal. This safe space is crucial for effective spiritual and emotional support.

3. Encouraging Honest Dialogue: By maintaining confidentiality, chaplains encourage honest and open dialogue. This honesty is vital for addressing the underlying issues that individuals face and for facilitating genuine healing and growth.

Ethical Guidelines for Confidentiality:

Chaplains adhere to strict ethical guidelines regarding confidentiality, which are often outlined by professional organizations and religious bodies. These guidelines help chaplains navigate complex situations and ensure that they uphold their ethical responsibilities.

Challenges in Maintaining Confidentiality

Institutional Constraints:

1. Security Concerns: Correctional facilities have strict security protocols that can sometimes conflict with the principle of confidentiality. Chaplains must navigate these protocols while maintaining trust with inmates.

2. Mandatory Reporting: Chaplains are often required to report certain information, such as threats of harm or illegal activities. Balancing mandatory reporting requirements with the commitment to confidentiality can be challenging.

Dual Loyalties:

Chaplains may experience dual loyalties—to the inmates they serve and the correctional institution that employs them. This duality can create ethical dilemmas, especially when the interests of inmates and the institution diverge.

Building Trust in a Distrustful Environment:

Correctional facilities are environments where trust is often in short supply. Inmates may be wary of sharing personal information due to past experiences of betrayal or exploitation. Chaplains must work diligently to overcome this distrust and establish a reliable and safe relationship.

Strategies for Building and Maintaining Trust

Transparency and Honesty:

1. Clear Communication: Chaplains should clearly communicate the boundaries of confidentiality to those they serve. This includes explaining what can and cannot be kept confidential due to legal and institutional requirements.

2. Honesty About Limitations: Being honest about the limitations of confidentiality helps manage expectations and builds credibility. Individuals are more likely to trust chaplains who are transparent about the constraints they face.

Consistent Ethical Practice:

1. Adhering to Ethical Standards: Consistently adhering to ethical standards and guidelines reinforces trust. Chaplains must be unwavering in their commitment to confidentiality, even in challenging situations.

2. Respecting Privacy: Respecting the privacy of individuals by not sharing their personal information without explicit consent is crucial. This respect fosters a sense of safety and trust.

Building Relationships:

1. Active Listening: Actively listening to individuals without judgment or interruption shows respect and empathy. This practice helps build a rapport and fosters trust.

2. Empathy and Compassion: Demonstrating genuine empathy and compassion helps individuals feel understood

and valued. Chaplains who show that they care about the well-being of those they serve are more likely to build strong, trusting relationships.

Navigating Mandatory Reporting:

1. Explaining Obligations: Chaplains should explain their mandatory reporting obligations at the outset of their relationship with an individual. This transparency helps individuals understand the boundaries of confidentiality.

2. Balancing Care and Compliance: When mandatory reporting is necessary, chaplains should balance their legal obligations with their pastoral care responsibilities. This may involve providing additional support to the individual during the reporting process.

Case Studies in Confidentiality and Trust

Case Study 1: Balancing Confidentiality and Security:

Chaplain Michael worked with an inmate, David, who confided that he was feeling increasingly hostile towards another inmate. Michael faced the ethical dilemma of maintaining confidentiality versus the need to prevent potential violence. He chose to address David's feelings through counseling while also discreetly alerting security personnel to monitor the situation. Michael's careful handling of the situation maintained David's trust while ensuring the safety of the facility.

Case Study 2: Navigating Mandatory Reporting:

Chaplain Maria was counseling an inmate, Lisa, who disclosed plans to escape from the facility. Maria had to navigate the tension between maintaining confidentiality and fulfilling her mandatory reporting obligations. She informed Lisa about her duty to report and provided support throughout the process. Maria's transparency and continued care helped maintain Lisa's trust despite the reporting requirement.

Case Study 3: Building Trust in a Distrustful Environment:

Chaplain John encountered an inmate, Mark, who was initially reluctant to share personal information due to past experiences of betrayal. John built trust through consistent visits, active listening, and demonstrating genuine care. Over time, Mark began to open up, allowing John to provide more effective spiritual and emotional support. This relationship highlights the importance of patience and persistence in building trust.

The Impact of Confidentiality and Trust on Chaplaincy

Enhanced Effectiveness of Spiritual Care:

When individuals trust their chaplains and believe in the confidentiality of their interactions, they are more likely to seek help and fully engage in the spiritual care process. This engagement enhances the effectiveness of chaplaincy, leading to better outcomes for those served.

Improved Mental and Emotional Well-Being:

Trusting relationships and the assurance of confidentiality contribute to the mental and emotional well-being of individuals. Knowing that their disclosures are kept private and respected helps alleviate anxiety and fosters a sense of security and stability.

Positive Institutional Relationships:

Chaplains who navigate the balance between confidentiality and institutional obligations effectively can foster positive relationships with both inmates and correctional staff. These relationships enhance the overall environment of the correctional facility, promoting mutual respect and cooperation.

Confidentiality and trust are cornerstones of effective chaplaincy, particularly in correctional settings. Maintaining these principles requires a delicate balance of ethical integrity, transparency, and empathy. By adhering to strict ethical standards, clearly communicating the boundaries of confidentiality, and building trusting relationships through consistent, compassionate care, chaplains can provide meaningful support to those they serve.

Boundary Setting: Establishing and Respecting Boundaries in Chaplaincy Practice

Establishing and respecting boundaries is a fundamental aspect of chaplaincy practice. Boundaries ensure that chaplains maintain professional integrity, foster trust, and provide effective spiritual care without compromising their ethical responsibilities. In correctional chaplaincy, where the dynamics can be particularly challenging, clear boundaries are essential for the safety and well-being of both chaplains and those they serve. This chapter explores the importance of boundary setting, common challenges, and strategies for maintaining appropriate boundaries in chaplaincy practice.

Understanding the Importance of Boundaries

Defining Boundaries in Chaplaincy:

Boundaries in chaplaincy refer to the ethical and professional limits that define the relationship between chaplains and those they serve. These boundaries protect both parties and ensure that the chaplaincy relationship remains focused on providing spiritual care.

The Role of Boundaries:

1. Professional Integrity: Boundaries help maintain the professional integrity of chaplains, ensuring that their actions are guided by ethical standards and best practices.

2. Trust and Safety: Clear boundaries foster trust and create a safe environment for individuals seeking spiritual care. They help prevent misunderstandings, exploitation, and emotional harm.

3. Effective Care: Boundaries enable chaplains to provide effective care by keeping the focus on the needs of those they serve, rather than on personal or inappropriate relationships.

Common Boundary Challenges in Chaplaincy

Emotional Attachment:

Chaplains often form close, empathetic relationships with those they serve. However, emotional attachment can lead to blurred boundaries, making it difficult to maintain professional distance and objectivity.

Dual Relationships:

Dual relationships occur when chaplains have multiple roles with the same individual, such as being both a spiritual advisor and a friend. These relationships can complicate the chaplaincy dynamic and create conflicts of interest.

Gifts and Favors:

Accepting gifts or favors from those receiving spiritual care can compromise the professional relationship. It may create a sense of obligation or favoritism, undermining the chaplain's impartiality.

Confidentiality and Over-Sharing:

Maintaining confidentiality is crucial, but chaplains must also be careful not to over-share personal information with those they serve. Over-sharing can shift the focus away from the individual's needs and blur professional boundaries.

Strategies for Establishing and Maintaining Boundaries

Education and Training:

1. Boundary Training: Regular training on boundary setting and ethical guidelines helps chaplains understand the importance of boundaries and how to maintain them.

2. Case Studies: Reviewing case studies and ethical dilemmas provides practical insights into boundary challenges and effective strategies for addressing them.

Clear Communication:

1. Setting Expectations: Chaplains should clearly communicate the boundaries of their role at the outset of their relationship with an individual. This includes explaining the limits of confidentiality and the nature of their support.

2. Consistent Messaging: Consistently reinforcing boundaries through actions and words helps prevent misunderstandings and reinforces the professional nature of the chaplaincy relationship.

Supervision and Accountability:

1. Regular Supervision: Engaging in regular supervision with experienced colleagues or supervisors provides chaplains with guidance and support in maintaining boundaries.

2. Peer Support: Participating in peer support groups allows chaplains to discuss boundary issues, share experiences, and seek advice from peers.

Self-Reflection and Self-Care:

1. Reflective Practice: Chaplains should engage in regular self-reflection to assess their relationships and identify any potential boundary issues. Reflective practice helps maintain self-awareness and professional integrity.

2. Self-Care: Prioritizing self-care helps chaplains manage their own emotional well-being, reducing the risk of burnout and maintaining the capacity to set and uphold boundaries.

Policies and Procedures:

1. Institutional Guidelines: Adhering to institutional policies and procedures on boundary setting provides a framework for ethical practice. Chaplains should be familiar with and follow these guidelines.

2. Ethical Codes: Professional ethical codes provide clear guidelines on boundary issues. Chaplains should be well-versed in these codes and incorporate them into their practice.

Case Studies in Boundary Setting

Case Study 1: Managing Emotional Attachment:

Chaplain Emily developed a close relationship with an inmate, Sarah, who was struggling with grief and trauma. Emily noticed that she was becoming emotionally attached to Sarah, which was affecting her objectivity. She sought supervision and discussed her feelings, receiving guidance on how to maintain professional distance while providing empathetic support. Emily's self-awareness and proactive approach helped her manage her emotional attachment and continue to provide effective care.

Case Study 2: Navigating Dual Relationships:

Chaplain Michael encountered a situation where an inmate, John, requested spiritual guidance and later asked Michael to intervene in a personal dispute with another inmate. Michael recognized the potential for a dual relationship and clearly communicated his role and boundaries to John. He provided spiritual support but referred John to appropriate resources for resolving the personal dispute. This approach maintained professional boundaries and avoided conflicts of interest.

Case Study 3: Handling Gifts and Favors:

Chaplain David was offered a handmade gift by an inmate, Mark, as a token of appreciation for his support. David kindly explained that accepting gifts could compromise their professional relationship and declined the gift. He expressed gratitude for the gesture and reinforced the importance of maintaining boundaries. David's respectful handling of the situation preserved the integrity of their relationship.

Case Study 4: Balancing Confidentiality and Over-Sharing:

Chaplain Maria found herself sharing personal stories with inmates to build rapport and trust. She realized that over-sharing was shifting the focus away from the inmates' needs. Maria reflected on her practice and sought supervision to address this issue. She learned to balance sharing relatable experiences without over-sharing, ensuring that the focus remained on providing spiritual care.

The Impact of Effective Boundary Setting

Enhanced Trust and Safety:

By establishing and maintaining clear boundaries, chaplains create a safe and trustworthy environment for individuals seeking spiritual care. This trust is crucial for effective counseling and support.

Professional Integrity:

Adhering to boundaries ensures that chaplains maintain their professional integrity and ethical standards. This integrity is essential for the credibility and effectiveness of chaplaincy practice.

Effective Care and Support:

Clear boundaries enable chaplains to focus on the needs of those they serve, providing effective and compassionate care. Boundaries help prevent burnout and ensure that chaplains can sustain their practice over the long term.

Positive Institutional Relationships:

Chaplains who maintain boundaries contribute to a positive institutional environment. Their professionalism and ethical conduct enhance the overall reputation of the chaplaincy program and foster cooperation with correctional staff.

Boundary setting is a critical aspect of chaplaincy practice, particularly in correctional settings. Establishing and respecting boundaries ensures professional integrity, fosters trust, and enables effective spiritual care. By engaging in education and training, clear communication, supervision, self-reflection, and adherence to ethical guidelines, chaplains can navigate the complexities of boundary issues and maintain the highest standards of ethical practice.

Cultural Competence: The Importance of Understanding and Respecting Diverse Cultural Backgrounds

Cultural competence is a critical component of effective chaplaincy, especially in correctional settings where inmates come from diverse cultural, religious, and ethnic backgrounds. Chaplains must navigate these differences with sensitivity and respect to provide meaningful spiritual care and support. This chapter explores the importance of cultural competence, the challenges chaplains face, and strategies for developing and maintaining cultural competence in chaplaincy practice.

Understanding Cultural Competence

Defining Cultural Competence:

Cultural competence refers to the ability to understand, appreciate, and interact with people from cultures or belief systems different from one's own. It involves recognizing and respecting cultural differences, being aware of one's own cultural biases, and adapting practices to meet the diverse needs of those served.

The Role of Cultural Competence in Chaplaincy:

1. Effective Communication: Cultural competence enhances communication by ensuring that chaplains understand and respect the cultural contexts of those they serve.

2. Building Trust: Respecting cultural differences fosters trust and rapport, making individuals more comfortable seeking and receiving spiritual care.

3. Providing Inclusive Care: Culturally competent chaplains can tailor their support to meet the unique needs of individuals from diverse backgrounds, ensuring that care is inclusive and respectful.

The Importance of Cultural Competence in Correctional Settings

Diverse Inmate Populations:

Correctional facilities house individuals from a wide range of cultural, ethnic, and religious backgrounds. Cultural competence is essential for chaplains to provide relevant and respectful support to this diverse population.

Addressing Cultural Barriers:

Cultural barriers can hinder effective communication and support. Chaplains must be equipped to identify and overcome these barriers to ensure that all individuals receive the care they need.

Promoting Inclusivity and Respect:

Cultural competence promotes an inclusive and respectful environment within correctional facilities. By understanding and valuing cultural differences, chaplains contribute to a more harmonious and supportive community.

Challenges in Developing Cultural Competence

Personal Biases:

Chaplains, like all individuals, have their own cultural biases and assumptions. Recognizing and addressing these biases is crucial for developing cultural competence.

Lack of Cultural Knowledge:

Chaplains may not be familiar with all the cultural practices and beliefs of the diverse populations they serve. This lack of knowledge can hinder their ability to provide effective support.

Navigating Conflicting Beliefs:

Chaplains may encounter situations where their own beliefs conflict with those of the individuals they serve. Navigating these conflicts while maintaining respect and professionalism can be challenging.

Strategies for Developing and Maintaining Cultural Competence

Education and Training:

1. Cultural Awareness Training: Participating in cultural awareness training helps chaplains understand the cultural backgrounds and practices of the populations they serve. This training should be ongoing to keep up with the changing demographics and needs.

2. Language Skills: Learning key phrases or terms in the languages spoken by inmates can enhance communication and demonstrate respect for their cultural backgrounds.

Self-Reflection and Awareness:

1. Reflective Practice: Engaging in regular self-reflection helps chaplains identify and address their own cultural biases and assumptions. Reflective practice fosters greater self-awareness and sensitivity.

2. Seeking Feedback: Chaplains should seek feedback from those they serve and from colleagues to understand how their actions and attitudes are perceived. This feedback can provide valuable insights for improving cultural competence.

Building Relationships:

1. Cultural Immersion: Building relationships with individuals from different cultural backgrounds allows chaplains to gain firsthand experience and understanding of their practices and beliefs.

2. Interfaith Collaboration: Working with religious leaders from various faith traditions promotes mutual understanding and respect. Interfaith collaboration enriches chaplaincy practice and ensures that diverse spiritual needs are met.

Adapting Practices:

1. Culturally Sensitive Counseling: Chaplains should adapt their counseling techniques to be culturally sensitive and relevant. This includes being aware of cultural norms regarding communication, privacy, and emotional expression.

2. Inclusive Worship Services: Organizing worship services that are inclusive of diverse religious practices fosters a sense of belonging and respect. Chaplains should consider incorporating elements from various traditions to accommodate the needs of all inmates.

Advocacy and Support:

1. Cultural Advocacy: Chaplains should advocate for the cultural and religious rights of inmates within the correctional facility. This includes ensuring access to culturally appropriate food, religious materials, and observance of cultural holidays.

2. Support Networks: Establishing support networks within and outside the correctional facility helps chaplains provide comprehensive care. Collaborating with community organizations and cultural groups enhances the resources available to inmates.

Case Studies in Cultural Competence

Case Study 1: Supporting Indigenous Spiritual Practices:

Chaplain Maria worked with an inmate, David, who was a member of a local Indigenous community. David expressed a desire to practice his traditional spiritual rituals, which were not initially supported by the facility. Maria advocated for David's right to practice his spirituality and arranged for a local Indigenous elder to visit and conduct ceremonies. This support was instrumental in David's spiritual well-being and highlighted the importance of cultural competence in chaplaincy.

Case Study 2: Navigating Religious Diversity:

Chaplain John served in a facility with a significant Muslim inmate population. To better support these inmates, John educated himself about Islamic practices and collaborated with a local imam to provide religious services and education. He also advocated for the provision of halal food and prayer spaces. John's efforts fostered a more inclusive environment and demonstrated respect for religious diversity.

Case Study 3: Addressing Language Barriers:

Chaplain Emily encountered several Spanish-speaking inmates who struggled to communicate their needs in English. Emily took the initiative to learn basic Spanish phrases and arranged for translation services when needed. She also provided religious materials in Spanish. These efforts significantly improved the inmates' access to spiritual care and support.

Case Study 4: Promoting Interfaith Understanding:

Chaplain David organized an interfaith dialogue program within the correctional facility, bringing together inmates from various religious backgrounds to share their beliefs and practices. This program promoted mutual respect and understanding, reducing tensions and fostering a sense of community. David's initiative highlighted the positive impact of cultural competence and interfaith collaboration.

The Impact of Cultural Competence on Chaplaincy

Enhanced Spiritual Care:

Cultural competence enables chaplains to provide more effective and meaningful spiritual care. By understanding and respecting diverse cultural backgrounds, chaplains can better address the spiritual needs of the individuals they serve.

Building Trust and Rapport:

When chaplains demonstrate cultural competence, they build trust and rapport with inmates. This trust is crucial for effective counseling and support, fostering a more positive and collaborative relationship.

Promoting Inclusivity and Respect:

Cultural competence promotes an inclusive and respectful environment within correctional facilities. Chaplains who value and respect cultural diversity contribute to a more harmonious and supportive community.

Improving Outcomes:

Culturally competent chaplaincy leads to better outcomes for inmates, including enhanced well-being, personal growth, and successful reintegration into society. By addressing the cultural and spiritual needs of inmates, chaplains support their rehabilitation and transformation.

Cultural competence is essential for effective chaplaincy practice, particularly in the diverse environment of correctional facilities. By understanding and respecting diverse cultural backgrounds, chaplains can provide meaningful spiritual care, build trust, and promote inclusivity. Developing and maintaining cultural competence requires ongoing education, self-reflection, relationship-building, and advocacy.

Professional Integrity: Upholding Professional Standards and Ethical Guidelines

Professional integrity is a cornerstone of effective chaplaincy. Upholding professional standards and ethical guidelines ensures that chaplains provide high-quality, respectful, and responsible care to those they serve. This chapter explores the importance of professional integrity in chaplaincy, the key standards and ethical guidelines that chaplains must adhere to, and strategies for maintaining professional integrity in practice.

The Importance of Professional Integrity

Defining Professional Integrity:

Professional integrity refers to the adherence to moral and ethical principles, honesty, and consistency in upholding professional standards. For chaplains, it involves maintaining the highest levels of ethical conduct in their interactions and responsibilities.

The Role of Professional Integrity in Chaplaincy:

1. Building Trust: Professional integrity fosters trust between chaplains and those they serve. Trust is essential for effective spiritual care and counseling.

2. Ensuring Quality Care: Upholding professional standards ensures that chaplains provide consistent, high-quality care that respects the dignity and rights of individuals.

3. Maintaining Ethical Conduct: Adhering to ethical guidelines protects chaplains and those they serve from potential harm and misconduct.

Key Standards and Ethical Guidelines in Chaplaincy

Professional Codes of Ethics:

Chaplains often adhere to codes of ethics provided by professional organizations such as the Association of Professional Chaplains (APC), National Association of Catholic Chaplains (NACC), and others. These codes outline the fundamental ethical principles and standards of practice for chaplains.

Confidentiality:

1. Respecting Privacy: Chaplains must maintain confidentiality to respect the privacy of those they serve. This includes not disclosing personal information without consent, except in cases where disclosure is legally mandated.

2. Building Trust: Confidentiality is crucial for building trust and ensuring that individuals feel safe sharing personal and sensitive information.

Boundaries:

1. Maintaining Professional Boundaries: Chaplains must establish and maintain appropriate professional boundaries to avoid dual relationships, conflicts of interest, and exploitation.

2. Preventing Harm: Clear boundaries protect both chaplains and those they serve from emotional, psychological, and physical harm.

Cultural Competence:

1. Respecting Diversity: Chaplains must demonstrate cultural competence by respecting and valuing the diverse cultural, religious, and ethnic backgrounds of those they serve.

2. Providing Inclusive Care: Cultural competence ensures that chaplains provide inclusive and respectful care that meets the unique needs of individuals from diverse backgrounds.

Integrity and Honesty:

1. Honest Communication: Chaplains must communicate honestly and transparently with those they serve, avoiding deception or misrepresentation.

2. Ethical Decision-Making: Integrity involves making ethical decisions that prioritize the well-being and rights of individuals, even in challenging situations.

Accountability:

1. Responsibility for Actions: Chaplains must take responsibility for their actions and decisions, being accountable to those they serve, their colleagues, and their professional organizations.

2. Continuous Improvement: Accountability involves a commitment to continuous improvement and professional development to enhance the quality of care provided.

Strategies for Maintaining Professional Integrity

Education and Training:

1. Ongoing Professional Development: Chaplains should engage in continuous education and training to stay updated on ethical guidelines, best practices, and emerging issues in chaplaincy.

2. Ethics Training: Participating in ethics training programs helps chaplains deepen their understanding of ethical principles and how to apply them in practice.

Self-Reflection and Supervision:

1. Reflective Practice: Regular self-reflection helps chaplains assess their actions and decisions, identify areas for improvement, and maintain ethical conduct.

2. Supervision and Peer Support: Engaging in supervision and peer support provides chaplains with guidance, feedback, and support in navigating ethical dilemmas and maintaining professional integrity.

Adherence to Ethical Guidelines:

1. Following Codes of Ethics: Chaplains should be familiar with and adhere to the ethical guidelines provided by their professional organizations. These guidelines serve as a foundation for ethical practice.

2. Institutional Policies: Chaplains must also follow the ethical policies and procedures of the institutions where they work, ensuring alignment with organizational standards.

Transparent Communication:

1. Setting Clear Expectations: Clearly communicating the scope and boundaries of chaplaincy services helps manage expectations and prevents misunderstandings.

2. Open Dialogue: Maintaining open and honest dialogue with those served, colleagues, and supervisors fosters transparency and trust.

Ethical Decision-Making:

1. Applying Ethical Frameworks: Using ethical frameworks and principles, such as beneficence, non-maleficence, autonomy, and justice, helps chaplains make well-rounded ethical decisions.

2. Seeking Guidance: In complex situations, chaplains should seek guidance from supervisors, ethics committees, or professional organizations to navigate ethical dilemmas effectively.

Case Studies in Professional Integrity

Case Study 1: Upholding Confidentiality:

Chaplain Sarah was approached by an inmate, James, who disclosed personal information about his mental health struggles. Sarah was later asked by a correctional officer about James's well-being. She explained that she could not disclose specific details due to confidentiality but encouraged the officer to refer James to appropriate mental health services. Sarah's adherence to confidentiality built trust with James and demonstrated her commitment to ethical practice.

Case Study 2: Maintaining Professional Boundaries:

Chaplain David developed a close rapport with an inmate, Lisa, who sought his counsel regularly. Lisa later invited David to attend her family event after her release. David respectfully declined, explaining the importance of maintaining professional boundaries to ensure the integrity of their chaplaincy relationship. His decision reinforced the professional nature of their interactions and upheld ethical standards.

Case Study 3: Demonstrating Cultural Competence:

Chaplain Maria served in a facility with a diverse inmate population, including many from different religious backgrounds. She made an effort to learn about various religious practices and collaborated with local religious leaders to provide inclusive spiritual services. Maria's commitment to cultural competence enhanced the quality of care and fostered a more inclusive environment.

Case Study 4: Ethical Decision-Making:

Chaplain John faced a dilemma when an inmate, Mark, expressed intentions to harm himself. John had to balance confidentiality with his duty to protect Mark's safety. He sought guidance from his supervisor and decided to report the risk to the appropriate authorities while continuing to provide support to Mark. John's decision prioritized Mark's well-being and demonstrated ethical decision-making in practice.

The Impact of Professional Integrity on Chaplaincy

Enhanced Trust and Respect:

Upholding professional standards and ethical guidelines builds trust and respect between chaplains and those they serve. Trust is essential for effective spiritual care and counseling.

High-Quality Care:

Adhering to ethical guidelines ensures that chaplains provide consistent, high-quality care that respects the dignity and rights of individuals. This quality of care supports the overall well-being of those served.

Positive Professional Relationships:

Professional integrity fosters positive relationships with colleagues, supervisors, and the broader institutional community. These relationships enhance collaboration and support the chaplain's role within the institution.

Ethical and Moral Leadership:

Chaplains who uphold professional integrity serve as ethical and moral leaders within their institutions. Their commitment to ethical practice sets a positive example and promotes a culture of respect and accountability.

Professional integrity is fundamental to the practice of chaplaincy. Upholding professional standards and ethical guidelines ensures that chaplains provide high-quality, respectful, and responsible care to those they serve. By engaging in ongoing education, self-reflection, transparent communication, and ethical decision-making, chaplains can maintain the highest standards of professional integrity.

CHAPTER 09

THE FUTURE OF CHAPLAINCY

Emerging Trends: New Developments and Innovations in Chaplaincy

The field of chaplaincy is continually evolving to meet the changing needs of society and the individuals it serves. Emerging trends and innovations are shaping the future of chaplaincy, enhancing its relevance and effectiveness in various contexts, including correctional facilities, healthcare, education, and corporate environments. This chapter explores these new developments, highlighting how they are transforming the practice of chaplaincy and what they mean for the future of the profession.

Technological Advancements

Telechaplaincy and Virtual Support:

1. Expanding Access: Telechaplaincy uses video conferencing and online platforms to provide spiritual care to individuals who may not have access to in-person chaplaincy services. This innovation expands the reach of chaplaincy, particularly in remote or underserved areas.

2. Virtual Support Groups: Online support groups and faith communities offer a space for individuals to connect, share experiences, and receive spiritual guidance from chaplains. These virtual groups provide continuity of care and community support.

Digital Resources:

1. Mobile Apps: Mobile applications designed for spiritual growth, meditation, prayer, and ethical decision-making are becoming increasingly popular. These apps offer users easy access to chaplaincy resources and support.

2. Online Educational Programs: Digital platforms provide access to religious education and training programs. Chaplains can use these platforms to deliver courses, workshops, and seminars to a broader audience.

Integrative and Holistic Approaches

Holistic Care Models:

1. Mind-Body-Spirit Integration: Chaplains are increasingly adopting holistic care models that integrate physical, emotional, and spiritual well-being. This approach

recognizes the interconnectedness of various aspects of health and aims to provide comprehensive care.

2. Interdisciplinary Collaboration: Collaborating with healthcare providers, mental health professionals, and social workers, chaplains play a vital role in interdisciplinary care teams. This collaboration enhances the overall effectiveness of care by addressing the diverse needs of individuals.

Trauma-Informed Care:

1. Understanding Trauma: Chaplains are receiving training in trauma-informed care to better understand the impact of trauma on individuals and provide appropriate support. This approach emphasizes safety, trustworthiness, and empowerment.

2. Resilience and Recovery: Incorporating resilience-building practices, chaplains help individuals recover from trauma and develop coping strategies. These practices include mindfulness, meditation, and spiritual exercises.

Diversity and Inclusivity

Cultural and Religious Competence:

1. Inclusive Chaplaincy Services: Chaplains are becoming more attuned to the diverse cultural and religious backgrounds of those they serve. This includes providing services that respect and accommodate various beliefs and practices.

2.   Interfaith Dialogue: Promoting interfaith understanding and collaboration, chaplains facilitate dialogue and cooperation among individuals from different religious traditions. This fosters a more inclusive and harmonious environment.

Gender and Sexuality Inclusivity:

1. LGBTQ+ Support: Chaplains are increasingly recognizing the unique needs of LGBTQ+ individuals and providing affirming and inclusive spiritual care. This includes creating safe spaces and advocating for their rights within institutions.

2. Gender Sensitivity: Addressing gender-related issues with sensitivity, chaplains support individuals in navigating their spiritual journeys in ways that respect their gender identities and experiences.

Innovative Programs and Practices

Restorative Justice Initiatives:

1. Healing and Reconciliation: Chaplains are leading restorative justice programs that focus on healing and reconciliation between offenders and victims. These initiatives promote accountability, forgiveness, and community restoration.

2. Victim-Offender Dialogues: Facilitating dialogues between victims and offenders, chaplains help both parties

find closure and understanding. These conversations are structured to promote empathy and healing.

Spiritual Entrepreneurship:

1. Community-Based Programs: Chaplains are developing community-based programs that address social issues such as homelessness, addiction, and poverty. These programs often combine spiritual support with practical assistance.

2. Social Enterprises: Some chaplains are involved in creating social enterprises that provide employment and training opportunities for marginalized populations. These initiatives aim to empower individuals and promote economic justice.

Research and Evidence-Based Practice

Evidence-Based Chaplaincy:

1. Research Studies: Increasingly, chaplains are participating in research studies to demonstrate the impact and effectiveness of their work. This research helps build an evidence base that supports the value of chaplaincy services.

2. Outcome Measurement: Developing and utilizing tools to measure the outcomes of chaplaincy interventions, chaplains can provide data on the benefits of spiritual care. This includes assessing improvements in well-being, mental health, and spiritual growth.

Best Practices and Standards:

1. Professional Standards: Establishing and adhering to best practices and professional standards ensures the quality and consistency of chaplaincy services. Professional organizations play a key role in defining and promoting these standards.

2. Continuous Improvement: Chaplains are committed to continuous improvement, regularly updating their skills and knowledge to stay current with emerging trends and best practices in the field.

Global Perspectives and Collaborations

International Chaplaincy:

1. Global Networks: Chaplains are increasingly engaging in global networks and collaborations to share knowledge, resources, and best practices. These networks enhance the professional development of chaplains worldwide.

2. Cross-Cultural Training: Participating in cross-cultural training programs, chaplains gain insights into different cultural and religious contexts, improving their ability to provide relevant and respectful care.

Humanitarian and Disaster Response:

1. Emergency Chaplaincy: Chaplains are playing a crucial role in humanitarian and disaster response efforts, providing spiritual and emotional support to those affected by

crises. Their presence helps communities cope with trauma and loss.

2. Partnerships with NGOs: Collaborating with non-governmental organizations (NGOs) and international aid agencies, chaplains contribute to comprehensive relief efforts, addressing both physical and spiritual needs.

Case Studies in Emerging Trends

Case Study 1: Telechaplaincy in Correctional Facilities:

Chaplain Sarah implemented a telechaplaincy program in a rural correctional facility where access to in-person chaplaincy services was limited. Using video conferencing technology, she provided regular spiritual counseling and facilitated virtual support groups. The program significantly improved inmates' access to spiritual care and reduced feelings of isolation.

Case Study 2: Integrative Holistic Care in Healthcare:

Chaplain David worked in a hospital setting where he collaborated with doctors, nurses, and mental health professionals to provide holistic care to patients. By addressing the physical, emotional, and spiritual needs of patients, the interdisciplinary team improved overall patient outcomes and satisfaction.

Case Study 3: Restorative Justice in a Juvenile Detention Center:

Chaplain Maria led a restorative justice program in a juvenile detention center, facilitating dialogues between young offenders and their victims. These dialogues promoted accountability and empathy, helping the juveniles understand the impact of their actions and encouraging positive behavioral change.

Case Study 4: LGBTQ+ Inclusivity in Chaplaincy Services:

Chaplain John developed an LGBTQ+ inclusivity program within his chaplaincy practice, providing specialized support groups and advocacy for LGBTQ+ inmates. His efforts created a more inclusive environment and helped address the unique spiritual needs of LGBTQ+ individuals.

The field of chaplaincy is undergoing significant transformation, driven by technological advancements, integrative care models, and a commitment to diversity and inclusivity. Emerging trends and innovations are enhancing the relevance and effectiveness of chaplaincy, ensuring that chaplains can meet the evolving needs of the individuals and communities they serve.

Technology and Chaplaincy: The Role of Technology in Enhancing Chaplaincy Services

Technology is increasingly playing a transformative role in chaplaincy, enabling chaplains to provide more accessible, efficient, and effective spiritual care. This chapter explores the various ways technology is enhancing chaplaincy services, including the use of telechaplaincy, digital resources, online training, and data analytics. It also addresses the challenges and opportunities that come with integrating technology into chaplaincy practice.

The Rise of Telechaplaincy

Telechaplaincy and Virtual Support:

1. Expanding Access: Telechaplaincy utilizes video conferencing, phone calls, and online platforms to provide spiritual care to individuals who may not have access to in-person chaplaincy services. This is particularly beneficial in remote areas, for individuals with mobility issues, and during times of crisis, such as the COVID-19 pandemic.

2. Virtual Support Groups: Online support groups and virtual faith communities offer a space for individuals to connect, share experiences, and receive spiritual guidance from chaplains. These virtual groups provide continuity of care and a sense of community for participants who might otherwise feel isolated.

Case Study: Telechaplaincy in Correctional Facilities:

Chaplain Lisa implemented a telechaplaincy program in a rural correctional facility where access to in-person chaplaincy services was limited. Using video conferencing technology, she provided regular spiritual counseling and facilitated virtual support groups. The program significantly improved inmates' access to spiritual care and reduced feelings of isolation.

Digital Resources and Tools

Mobile Apps:

1. Spiritual Growth Apps: Mobile applications designed for spiritual growth, meditation, prayer, and ethical decision-making are becoming increasingly popular. These apps offer users easy access to chaplaincy resources and support, helping them maintain their spiritual practices on the go.

2. Chaplaincy Support Apps: Apps tailored specifically for chaplains provide tools for scheduling appointments, managing caseloads, and accessing resources for spiritual care. These apps enhance the efficiency and effectiveness of chaplaincy services.

Online Educational Programs:

1. Digital Training Platforms: Digital platforms provide access to religious education and training programs for chaplains and those they serve. Chaplains can use these

platforms to deliver courses, workshops, and seminars to a broader audience.

2. E-Learning Modules: E-learning modules on topics such as ethics, cultural competence, and trauma-informed care offer chaplains the opportunity to continue their professional development and stay updated on best practices.

Case Study: Mobile Apps for Spiritual Care:

Chaplain Michael recommended a spiritual growth app to inmates in a correctional facility. The app included daily meditation exercises, prayer prompts, and ethical reflections. Inmates reported that the app helped them stay connected to their spiritual practices and provided a sense of peace and structure.

Data Analytics and Outcome Measurement

Evidence-Based Chaplaincy:

1. Research and Data Collection: Increasingly, chaplains are participating in research studies and collecting data to demonstrate the impact and effectiveness of their work. This research helps build an evidence base that supports the value of chaplaincy services.

2. Outcome Measurement Tools: Developing and utilizing tools to measure the outcomes of chaplaincy interventions, chaplains can provide data on the benefits of

spiritual care. This includes assessing improvements in well-being, mental health, and spiritual growth.

Case Study: Measuring the Impact of Spiritual Care:

Chaplain Sarah collaborated with a research team to develop a survey tool for measuring the impact of spiritual care on inmate well-being. The survey included questions on emotional health, spiritual growth, and overall satisfaction with chaplaincy services. The data collected demonstrated significant positive outcomes, supporting the value of chaplaincy in the correctional facility.

Challenges and Opportunities

Challenges:

1. Digital Divide: Access to technology can be limited for some populations, including those in rural areas or low-income settings. Chaplains must find ways to bridge the digital divide and ensure that technology does not exacerbate existing inequalities.

2. Confidentiality and Privacy: Maintaining confidentiality and privacy in digital communications can be challenging. Chaplains must use secure platforms and follow best practices to protect the personal information of those they serve.

3. Training and Adaptation: Chaplains need training to effectively use new technologies. Adapting to technological advancements requires ongoing education and support.

Opportunities:

1. Enhanced Accessibility: Technology makes chaplaincy services more accessible to individuals who might otherwise have limited access. This includes people in remote locations, those with disabilities, and individuals in correctional facilities.

2. Increased Efficiency: Digital tools streamline administrative tasks, allowing chaplains to focus more on direct care. This increases the efficiency and effectiveness of chaplaincy services.

3. Broader Reach: Online platforms and digital resources enable chaplains to reach a wider audience, providing spiritual care and education to people around the world.

Best Practices for Integrating Technology into Chaplaincy

Ensuring Accessibility:

1. Inclusive Design: When developing digital resources, ensure they are accessible to individuals with disabilities and those with limited digital literacy. This includes using user-friendly interfaces and providing alternative formats.

2. Bridging the Digital Divide: Work with organizations and community partners to provide access to

technology for underserved populations. This might include offering digital literacy training or providing devices and internet access.

Maintaining Confidentiality:

1. Secure Platforms: Use secure, encrypted platforms for digital communications to protect the confidentiality and privacy of those served.

2. Informed Consent: Obtain informed consent from individuals before using digital tools for spiritual care. Clearly explain the potential risks and benefits of digital communication.

Ongoing Training:

1. Professional Development: Participate in ongoing training and professional development to stay updated on technological advancements and best practices in digital chaplaincy.

2. Peer Support: Engage in peer support networks to share experiences, challenges, and strategies for integrating technology into chaplaincy practice.

Technology is playing an increasingly important role in enhancing chaplaincy services, offering new ways to provide spiritual care and support. From telechaplaincy and mobile apps to data analytics and online education, technological advancements are transforming the practice of chaplaincy, making it more accessible, efficient, and effective.

As chaplains embrace these new tools and approaches, they must also address the challenges and ethical considerations that come with integrating technology into their practice. By ensuring accessibility, maintaining confidentiality, and committing to ongoing training, chaplains can harness the power of technology to better serve their communities and enhance their impact.

Global Perspectives: The Expansion of Chaplaincy in Different Cultural and National Contexts

The practice of chaplaincy is expanding globally, adapting to diverse cultural and national contexts while addressing the unique spiritual, emotional, and ethical needs of different populations. This chapter explores the ways in which chaplaincy is evolving in various parts of the world, highlighting the challenges and opportunities that come with this expansion. It also examines the innovative approaches being adopted to make chaplaincy more relevant and effective in different cultural settings.

The Global Expansion of Chaplaincy

Historical Context:

Chaplaincy has historically been rooted in specific religious traditions and cultural contexts, primarily within

Western countries. However, globalization and increasing cultural exchange have led to the spread and adaptation of chaplaincy practices worldwide.

Current Trends:

Today, chaplaincy is practiced in a variety of settings, including healthcare, education, the military, and correctional facilities, across many countries. The global expansion of chaplaincy reflects a growing recognition of the importance of spiritual care and the universal need for compassionate support.

Chaplaincy in Different Cultural Contexts

Africa:

1. Community-Based Chaplaincy: In many African countries, chaplaincy often involves community-based approaches that integrate traditional healing practices with modern spiritual care. Chaplains work closely with local leaders and communities to provide holistic support.

2. Challenges: Limited resources and access to training can hinder the development of chaplaincy programs. However, grassroots initiatives and international partnerships are helping to build capacity and enhance the effectiveness of chaplaincy services.

Asia:

1. Interfaith Collaboration: In culturally diverse regions such as India and Southeast Asia, chaplains frequently

engage in interfaith collaboration to address the spiritual needs of individuals from various religious backgrounds. This approach promotes mutual respect and understanding.

2. Innovative Practices: In countries like Japan, chaplaincy in healthcare settings often includes elements of mindfulness and Zen practices, reflecting the local cultural and religious context.

Europe:

1. Secular and Multicultural Contexts: European chaplaincy is increasingly operating within secular and multicultural societies. Chaplains must navigate diverse belief systems and provide inclusive care that respects both religious and non-religious perspectives.

2. Professional Standards: Europe has seen a push towards the professionalization of chaplaincy, with efforts to establish standardized training and certification programs across different countries.

Latin America:

1. Liberation Theology: In many Latin American countries, chaplaincy is influenced by liberation theology, which emphasizes social justice and the empowerment of marginalized communities. Chaplains often engage in advocacy and community development work.

2. Community Integration: Chaplains in Latin America frequently work within communities, addressing social and spiritual issues in tandem and fostering a sense of solidarity and collective action.

Middle East:

1. Islamic Chaplaincy: Islamic chaplaincy is becoming more recognized and institutionalized in countries like Saudi Arabia, UAE, and Egypt. Chaplains provide spiritual guidance in accordance with Islamic teachings and address the specific needs of Muslim populations.

2. Interfaith Dialogue: In areas with religious diversity, such as Lebanon, chaplains engage in interfaith dialogue to promote peace and understanding among different religious groups.

North America:

1. Diverse Settings: In the United States and Canada, chaplaincy services are provided in a wide range of settings, including hospitals, prisons, universities, and the military. Chaplains address the needs of diverse populations, including immigrants and refugees.

2. Focus on Inclusivity: There is a strong emphasis on inclusivity and cultural competence, with chaplains receiving training to support individuals from various cultural, religious, and ethnic backgrounds.

Challenges and Opportunities

Cultural Sensitivity and Adaptation:

1. Understanding Local Contexts: Chaplains must develop a deep understanding of the local cultural and religious contexts in which they work. This includes learning about traditional practices, beliefs, and social norms.

2. Adapting Practices: Effective chaplaincy requires adapting practices to be culturally relevant and respectful. This may involve integrating local spiritual practices and collaborating with traditional healers and religious leaders.

Training and Professional Development:

1. Access to Training: In many regions, access to formal chaplaincy training programs is limited. Efforts are being made to develop local training programs and create partnerships with international institutions to provide education and resources.

2. Professional Standards: Establishing professional standards and certification programs helps ensure the quality and consistency of chaplaincy services globally. This also enhances the credibility and recognition of chaplaincy as a profession.

Interfaith and Cross-Cultural Collaboration:

1. Building Bridges: Chaplains often serve as bridges between different cultural and religious groups, promoting dialogue and understanding. Interfaith and cross-cultural

collaboration are key to addressing the diverse needs of global populations.

2. Shared Learning: International conferences, workshops, and online platforms facilitate shared learning and exchange of best practices among chaplains from different cultural contexts.

Resource Constraints:

1. Funding and Support: Limited funding and resources can be a significant barrier to the development and sustainability of chaplaincy programs. Advocacy and fundraising efforts are crucial to securing the necessary support.

2. Technological Solutions: Leveraging technology, such as telechaplaincy and online training platforms, can help overcome some of the resource constraints and expand the reach of chaplaincy services.

Case Studies in Global Chaplaincy

Case Study 1: Community-Based Chaplaincy in Kenya:

Chaplain David works in a rural Kenyan village, providing spiritual care and support to the community. He integrates traditional healing practices with modern chaplaincy, collaborating with local elders and healers. This approach respects the community's cultural heritage while addressing their spiritual needs.

Case Study 2: Interfaith Chaplaincy in India:

Chaplain Anjali serves in a multicultural and multi-religious urban area in India. She facilitates interfaith dialogues and offers spiritual care to individuals from Hindu, Muslim, Christian, and Sikh backgrounds. Her work promotes mutual respect and understanding among the diverse religious communities.

Case Study 3: Islamic Chaplaincy in the UAE:

Chaplain Ahmed provides spiritual guidance in a hospital in the UAE, supporting Muslim patients and their families. He incorporates Islamic teachings into his care practices and collaborates with imams to ensure the spiritual needs of patients are met in accordance with their faith.

Case Study 4: Liberation Theology in Brazil:

Chaplain Maria is involved in a chaplaincy program in Brazil that focuses on social justice and community empowerment. Influenced by liberation theology, she works with marginalized communities, advocating for their rights and providing spiritual support that addresses both their social and spiritual needs.

Case Study 5: Secular and Multicultural Chaplaincy in Germany:

Chaplain Hans operates in a secular and multicultural context in Germany. He provides inclusive spiritual care that respects both religious and non-religious perspectives, adapting his practices to meet the diverse needs of the population he serves.

The global expansion of chaplaincy highlights the universal need for spiritual care and the adaptability of chaplaincy practices to diverse cultural and national contexts. Chaplains around the world are finding innovative ways to address the unique spiritual, emotional, and ethical needs of the populations they serve, despite the challenges they face.

As the field of chaplaincy continues to evolve globally, it is essential for chaplains to develop cultural sensitivity, engage in continuous professional development, and collaborate across cultural and religious boundaries. These efforts will ensure that chaplaincy remains relevant, effective, and inclusive, providing compassionate and meaningful support to individuals and communities worldwide.

Vision for the Future: Envisioning the Future of Chaplaincy and Its Continued Impact on Society

As we look to the future, the field of chaplaincy stands at a pivotal point of growth and transformation. The evolving needs of society, coupled with technological advancements and a deeper understanding of holistic care, present new opportunities for chaplains to expand their impact. This chapter explores a vision for the future of chaplaincy, highlighting the potential for its continued development and the ways in which it can enhance its contributions to individuals, communities, and society at large.

Integrating Holistic and Inclusive Care

Holistic Approaches:

1. Mind-Body-Spirit Integration: The future of chaplaincy will see a continued emphasis on holistic care, integrating physical, emotional, and spiritual well-being. Chaplains will collaborate with healthcare providers, mental health professionals, and social workers to offer comprehensive support.

2. Trauma-Informed Care: Training in trauma-informed care will become standard, enabling chaplains to provide sensitive and effective support to individuals who have experienced trauma.

Inclusivity and Diversity:

1. Cultural Competence: Chaplains will deepen their cultural competence, ensuring they can effectively serve diverse populations. This includes understanding and respecting various cultural, religious, and ethnic backgrounds.

2. LGBTQ+ Inclusivity: Chaplains will continue to develop programs and services that address the unique

spiritual needs of LGBTQ+ individuals, fostering an inclusive and supportive environment.

Technological Integration

Telechaplaincy and Digital Services:

1. Expanded Telechaplaincy: Telechaplaincy will become more widespread, offering spiritual care to individuals in remote areas, those with mobility issues, and during times of crisis. Virtual support groups and online faith communities will provide continuous care.

2. Mobile and Online Resources: The development of mobile apps and online platforms will offer accessible resources for spiritual growth, meditation, and ethical decision-making. Chaplains will utilize these tools to enhance their reach and effectiveness.

Data Analytics and Research:

1. Outcome Measurement: Chaplains will increasingly use data analytics to measure the impact of their services. This evidence-based approach will help demonstrate the value of chaplaincy and inform best practices.

2. Research Collaboration: Collaboration with academic institutions and research organizations will advance the field of chaplaincy, providing insights into its effectiveness and areas for improvement.

Professional Development and Standards

Enhanced Training Programs:

1. Interdisciplinary Training: Future training programs will emphasize interdisciplinary approaches, equipping chaplains with skills in healthcare, mental health, and social work. This comprehensive training will enable chaplains to address the multifaceted needs of those they serve.

2. Global Standards: Efforts to establish global standards for chaplaincy training and certification will ensure consistency and quality in chaplaincy services worldwide.

Ethical and Professional Integrity:

1. Ethical Guidelines: Chaplains will adhere to robust ethical guidelines, maintaining professional integrity and accountability. Ongoing education in ethics will be a key component of professional development.

2. Peer Support and Supervision: Regular peer support and supervision will provide chaplains with guidance and feedback, fostering continuous improvement and ethical practice.

Expanding Roles and Settings

Broader Applications:

1. Corporate Chaplaincy: The role of chaplains in corporate settings will expand, addressing the spiritual and emotional needs of employees and promoting ethical leadership.

2. Educational Institutions: Chaplains will play a larger role in schools and universities, supporting students' holistic development and fostering inclusive communities.

Innovative Programs:

1. Restorative Justice: Chaplains will lead restorative justice initiatives that focus on healing and reconciliation, both within correctional facilities and in broader community contexts.

2. Social Entrepreneurship: Chaplains will engage in social entrepreneurship, developing programs that address social issues such as homelessness, addiction, and poverty, and integrating spiritual care with practical support.

Global Collaboration and Impact

International Networks:

1. Global Collaboration: Chaplains will participate in international networks and collaborations, sharing knowledge, resources, and best practices. These global connections will enhance the professional development of chaplains and the effectiveness of their services.

2. Cross-Cultural Training: Cross-cultural training programs will prepare chaplains to work in diverse cultural contexts, improving their ability to provide relevant and respectful care.

Humanitarian Efforts:

1. Disaster Response: Chaplains will continue to play a crucial role in humanitarian and disaster response efforts, providing spiritual and emotional support to affected communities. Their presence will help individuals cope with trauma and rebuild their lives.

2. Partnerships with NGOs: Collaborating with non-governmental organizations (NGOs) and international aid agencies, chaplains will contribute to comprehensive relief efforts, addressing both physical and spiritual needs.

Visionary Leadership and Advocacy

Advocacy for Spiritual Care:

1. Policy Advocacy: Chaplains will advocate for policies that recognize the importance of spiritual care in healthcare, correctional systems, education, and other sectors. Their efforts will help integrate spiritual care into public health and social service frameworks.

2. Public Awareness: Raising public awareness about the value of chaplaincy will foster greater support and recognition. Chaplains will use media, public speaking, and community engagement to highlight their impact.

Visionary Leadership:

1. Innovative Leadership: Chaplains will take on visionary leadership roles, driving innovation and shaping the future of the profession. They will mentor the next generation

of chaplains and promote a forward-thinking approach to spiritual care.

2. Community Engagement: Engaging with communities and building strong relationships will be central to chaplaincy practice. Chaplains will work collaboratively with community leaders, faith groups, and organizations to address local needs and promote well-being.

The future of chaplaincy is one of growth, innovation, and expanded impact. By integrating holistic and inclusive care, embracing technological advancements, and maintaining professional integrity, chaplains will continue to provide vital spiritual and emotional support to diverse populations.

As chaplaincy evolves, it will play an increasingly important role in addressing the complex challenges of contemporary society. From corporate boardrooms to disaster-stricken communities, chaplains will offer compassion, guidance, and hope, making a profound difference in the lives of individuals and the health of communities.

The vision for the future of chaplaincy is bright, filled with opportunities for global collaboration, interdisciplinary integration, and visionary leadership. By embracing these opportunities and staying true to their ethical principles, chaplains will continue to enhance their contributions to society and fulfill their mission of providing compassionate, effective, and transformative spiritual care.

CONCLUSION

Chaplaincy remains a vital and dynamic field, providing essential spiritual, emotional, and ethical support across various contexts. This book has explored the rich history, foundational principles, and diverse applications of chaplaincy, highlighting its enduring relevance and transformative potential. Through detailed examination of its evolution, core principles, and the unique roles chaplains play in settings such as healthcare, correctional facilities, educational institutions, corporate environments, and diverse cultural contexts, we have seen how chaplaincy adapts to meet the changing needs of society.

The Timeless Value of Chaplaincy

From its ancient and medieval roots to its modern-day applications, chaplaincy has consistently offered a source of hope, comfort, and guidance. Chaplains have been present in times of war and peace, in moments of personal crisis and communal celebration, providing a steadfast presence that transcends the limitations of their immediate environments. Their work fosters resilience, promotes healing, and supports the ethical and spiritual development of individuals and communities.

Embracing Holistic and Inclusive Care

The shift towards holistic and inclusive care has underscored the importance of addressing the physical, emotional, and spiritual needs of those served. Chaplains are increasingly recognized as integral members of interdisciplinary teams, collaborating with healthcare providers, mental health professionals, and social workers to deliver comprehensive support. This approach not only enhances the quality of care but also ensures that diverse cultural and religious backgrounds are respected and valued.

Leveraging Technology for Greater Reach

Technological advancements have expanded the reach and effectiveness of chaplaincy services. Telechaplaincy, mobile apps, and digital resources have made spiritual care more accessible to individuals who might otherwise be underserved. These tools have also facilitated the collection of data and outcome measurement, helping to demonstrate the tangible benefits of chaplaincy and guide evidence-based practice.

Upholding Professional Standards and Ethical Integrity

The commitment to professional integrity remains a cornerstone of chaplaincy. Adhering to ethical guidelines, maintaining confidentiality, respecting boundaries, and pursuing continuous professional development ensure that chaplains uphold the highest standards of care. This dedication not only builds trust but also fosters a culture of respect and accountability within the institutions and communities they serve.

Expanding Roles and Global Impact

The expansion of chaplaincy into new roles and settings, including corporate environments and educational institutions, reflects its adaptability and relevance. As chaplains engage in innovative programs such as restorative justice and social entrepreneurship, they address pressing social issues and contribute to the well-being of diverse populations. The global perspective of chaplaincy highlights its universal applicability and the shared need for spiritual support across different cultural and national contexts.

Vision for the Future

Looking ahead, chaplaincy is poised for continued growth and transformation. The integration of holistic care models, technological innovations, and a commitment to inclusivity and diversity will enhance the impact of chaplaincy. Global collaboration, interdisciplinary training, and advocacy for spiritual care policies will further solidify the role of chaplains as essential providers of compassionate support.

A Closing Reflection

As we conclude this exploration of chaplaincy, it is evident that the field holds immense potential to transform lives and communities. Chaplains, with their dedication to service and unwavering commitment to ethical principles, will continue to be beacons of hope and compassion in a complex and ever-changing world.

The enduring relevance of chaplaincy lies in its ability to adapt to the needs of those it serves, offering a compassionate presence that transcends boundaries and fosters healing, growth, and resilience. As chaplaincy evolves, its core mission remains unchanged: to provide spiritual, emotional, and ethical support that nurtures the human spirit and uplifts the human condition.

In celebrating the rich history and future promise of chaplaincy, we acknowledge the profound impact of this vital field and the transformative potential it holds for individuals, communities, and society as a whole.

APPENDICES

Appendix A: Code of Ethics for Chaplains

The following Code of Ethics for Chaplains is designed to provide a framework for the ethical and professional conduct of chaplains in various settings. This code is intended to guide chaplains in their practice, ensuring that they uphold the highest standards of integrity, respect, and compassion in their service to individuals and communities.

1. Professional Conduct

1.1 Integrity:

Chaplains shall conduct themselves with integrity, honesty, and transparency in all professional relationships.

They shall be truthful in their communication and actions, avoiding any form of deception or misrepresentation.

1.2 Accountability:

Chaplains shall be accountable for their actions and decisions, taking responsibility for their professional conduct. They shall seek supervision and peer support to ensure their practice remains ethical and effective.

1.3 Competence:

Chaplains shall maintain high standards of competence in their professional practice. They shall engage in ongoing education and training to stay updated on best practices and emerging issues in chaplaincy.

1.4 Professional Boundaries:

Chaplains shall establish and maintain appropriate professional boundaries with those they serve. They shall avoid dual relationships, conflicts of interest, and any behavior that could compromise their professional integrity.

2. Respect for Persons

2.1 Dignity and Worth:

Chaplains shall respect the inherent dignity and worth of every person they serve. They shall treat all individuals with compassion, respect, and empathy, regardless of their background or circumstances.

2.2 Cultural Competence:

Chaplains shall demonstrate cultural competence, respecting and valuing the diverse cultural, religious, and ethnic backgrounds of those they serve. They shall strive to provide inclusive and relevant care that honors individual differences.

2.3 Autonomy:

Chaplains shall respect the autonomy and right to self-determination of individuals. They shall support individuals in making informed decisions about their own spiritual care and well-being.

3. Confidentiality

3.1 Privacy:

Chaplains shall protect the confidentiality of information shared by those they serve. They shall safeguard personal information and ensure that it is not disclosed without the individual's consent, except in cases where disclosure is legally mandated.

3.2 Informed Consent:

Chaplains shall obtain informed consent from individuals before sharing information or using technology for spiritual care. They shall clearly explain the limits of confidentiality and the potential risks and benefits of disclosure.

4. Ethical Practice

4.1 Non-Maleficence:

Chaplains shall do no harm in their practice. They shall act in the best interests of those they serve, avoiding actions that could cause physical, emotional, or spiritual harm.

4.2 Beneficence:

Chaplains shall actively promote the well-being of individuals and communities. They shall provide compassionate care that enhances the spiritual, emotional, and ethical growth of those they serve.

4.3 Justice:

Chaplains shall promote fairness and equity in their practice. They shall advocate for the rights and needs of marginalized and vulnerable populations, working to address social injustices and systemic inequalities.

5. Professional Relationships

5.1 Collaboration:

Chaplains shall collaborate with colleagues, supervisors, and other professionals to provide comprehensive and coordinated care. They shall seek to build positive and respectful relationships within their professional community.

5.2 Conflict Resolution:

Chaplains shall address conflicts in a respectful and constructive manner. They shall seek to resolve disputes through dialogue and mediation, promoting reconciliation and understanding.

5.3 Professional Development:

Chaplains shall engage in continuous professional development, seeking opportunities to enhance their skills and knowledge. They shall participate in supervision, peer support, and professional organizations to support their growth and effectiveness.

6. Advocacy and Social Responsibility

6.1 Advocacy:

Chaplains shall advocate for the spiritual and emotional needs of individuals and communities. They shall work to ensure that all individuals have access to appropriate spiritual care and support.

6.2 Social Responsibility:

Chaplains shall recognize their social responsibilities and work to promote the common good. They shall engage in activities that contribute to the well-being of society and address social issues that impact the communities they serve.

6.3 Environmental Stewardship:

Chaplains shall promote environmental stewardship and sustainability. They shall encourage practices that respect and protect the natural world, recognizing the interconnectedness of all life.

7. Accountability to the Code

7.1 Adherence to the Code:

Chaplains shall adhere to this Code of Ethics in their professional practice. They shall review and reflect on these ethical guidelines regularly to ensure their actions align with these standards.

7.2 Reporting Ethical Violations:

Chaplains shall report ethical violations to appropriate authorities. They shall take action to address unethical behavior within their professional community, upholding the integrity of the chaplaincy profession.

7.3 Commitment to Improvement:

Chaplains shall commit to continuous improvement in their ethical practice. They shall seek feedback, reflect on their experiences, and strive to enhance their ethical awareness and conduct.

This Code of Ethics serves as a foundational guide for chaplains, supporting their commitment to ethical practice and professional integrity. By adhering to these principles, chaplains can provide compassionate, respectful, and effective spiritual care that honors the dignity and worth of every individual.

Appendix B: Sample Chaplaincy Programs and Curricula

This appendix provides examples of chaplaincy programs and curricula designed to prepare chaplains for various settings, including healthcare, correctional facilities, educational institutions, and corporate environments. These sample programs outline key components, learning objectives, and suggested coursework to equip chaplains with the knowledge and skills necessary for effective spiritual care.

Sample Chaplaincy Program: Healthcare Chaplaincy

Program Overview:

The Healthcare Chaplaincy program is designed to prepare chaplains to provide spiritual care in hospitals, hospices, and other healthcare settings. The curriculum emphasizes holistic care, ethical decision-making, and interdisciplinary collaboration.

Learning Objectives:

1. Understand the unique spiritual needs of patients, families, and healthcare staff.

2. Develop skills in providing pastoral care in a clinical setting.

3. Learn to navigate ethical dilemmas in healthcare.

4. Gain proficiency in interdisciplinary teamwork and communication.

Suggested Coursework:

1. Introduction to Healthcare Chaplaincy: Overview of the role and responsibilities of healthcare chaplains.

2. Clinical Pastoral Education (CPE): Supervised clinical training with a focus on pastoral care skills.

3. Ethics in Healthcare: Exploration of ethical issues in medical settings, including end-of-life care, patient autonomy, and confidentiality.

4. Spiritual Assessment and Care Planning: Techniques for assessing spiritual needs and developing care plans.

5. Cultural Competence in Healthcare: Understanding and respecting diverse cultural and religious backgrounds in patient care.

6. Grief and Bereavement Counseling: Providing support to patients and families dealing with loss and grief.

7. Interdisciplinary Collaboration: Working effectively with healthcare teams to provide comprehensive care.

Sample Chaplaincy Program: Correctional Chaplaincy Program Overview:

The Correctional Chaplaincy program prepares chaplains to serve in prisons, jails, and other correctional facilities. The curriculum focuses on restorative justice, trauma-informed care, and ethical challenges unique to the correctional environment.

Learning Objectives:

1. Provide spiritual care to inmates, staff, and their families.

2. Understand the principles of restorative justice and their application in correctional settings.

3. Develop skills in trauma-informed care and crisis intervention.

4. Navigate ethical challenges in the correctional environment.

Suggested Coursework:

1. Introduction to Correctional Chaplaincy: Overview of the role and responsibilities of correctional chaplains.

2. Restorative Justice: Principles and practices of restorative justice, including victim-offender dialogues.

3. Trauma-Informed Care: Understanding the impact of trauma and providing trauma-sensitive support.

4. Ethical Challenges in Corrections: Navigating confidentiality, dual relationships, and other ethical issues.

5. Conflict Resolution and Mediation: Techniques for resolving conflicts and mediating disputes within the correctional facility.

6. Addiction and Recovery Counseling: Supporting inmates with addiction issues and facilitating recovery programs.

7. Spiritual Programs and Services: Developing and leading religious services, study groups, and spiritual programs for inmates.

Sample Chaplaincy Program: Educational Chaplaincy

Program Overview:

The Educational Chaplaincy program is designed for chaplains serving in schools, colleges, and universities. The curriculum emphasizes support for students' spiritual and emotional development, crisis intervention, and promoting an inclusive campus environment.

Learning Objectives:

1. Provide spiritual and emotional support to students, faculty, and staff.

2. Develop skills in crisis intervention and counseling.

3. Foster an inclusive and supportive campus environment.

4. Promote ethical and moral development within the educational community.

Suggested Coursework:

1. Introduction to Educational Chaplaincy: Overview of the role and responsibilities of educational chaplains.

2. Student Counseling and Support: Techniques for providing individual and group counseling to students.

3. Crisis Intervention: Responding to emergencies and providing immediate support during crises.

4. Promoting Inclusivity: Creating an inclusive campus environment that respects diverse cultural and religious backgrounds.

5. Ethical Development and Education: Facilitating discussions and programs on ethical decision-making and moral development.

6. Interfaith Dialogue: Promoting interfaith understanding and collaboration on campus.

7. Spiritual Life Programming: Developing and leading spiritual programs, retreats, and worship services for the campus community.

Sample Chaplaincy Program: Corporate Chaplaincy

Program Overview:

The Corporate Chaplaincy program prepares chaplains to serve in business and corporate environments. The curriculum focuses on employee well-being, ethical leadership, and fostering a positive workplace culture.

Learning Objectives:

1. Provide spiritual and emotional support to employees and management.

2. Promote ethical behavior and corporate responsibility.

3. Develop skills in conflict resolution and stress management.

4. Foster a positive and inclusive workplace culture.

Suggested Coursework:

1. Introduction to Corporate Chaplaincy: Overview of the role and responsibilities of corporate chaplains.

2. Employee Support and Counseling: Techniques for providing support to employees dealing with personal and professional challenges.

3. Ethical Leadership: Promoting ethical behavior and corporate responsibility through chaplaincy.

4. Stress Management and Well-Being: Supporting employees' mental and emotional well-being.

5. Conflict Resolution in the Workplace: Techniques for mediating and resolving conflicts among employees and management.

6. Workplace Spirituality: Developing programs and initiatives that integrate spirituality into the workplace.

7. Cultural Competence in Corporate Settings: Understanding and respecting diversity in the corporate environment.

These sample chaplaincy programs and curricula provide a framework for preparing chaplains to serve effectively in various settings. By focusing on key learning objectives and providing relevant coursework, these programs equip chaplains with the knowledge and skills necessary to meet the spiritual, emotional, and ethical needs of those they serve. As the field of chaplaincy continues to evolve, these programs will adapt to incorporate new developments and best practices, ensuring that chaplains remain well-prepared to provide compassionate and effective care.

Appendix C: Resources for Further Reading

This appendix provides a curated list of resources for further reading, designed to deepen your understanding of chaplaincy and its various applications. These books, articles, and online resources cover a wide range of topics, including the history of chaplaincy, ethical guidelines, cultural competence, and innovative practices in different settings.

Books

1. "The Art of Pastoring: Ministry Without All the Answers" by David Hansen

   - A practical guide to pastoral care that emphasizes the importance of presence and listening in ministry.

2. "Chaplaincy: A Very Short Introduction" by Naomi K. Paget and Janet R. McCormack

   - An accessible overview of chaplaincy, exploring its history, roles, and ethical considerations.

3. "Professional Spiritual & Pastoral Care: A Practical Clergy and Chaplain's Handbook" edited by Rabbi Stephen B. Roberts

- A comprehensive handbook for chaplains and clergy, covering various aspects of spiritual care and pastoral counseling.

4. "The Wounded Healer: Ministry in Contemporary Society" by Henri J.M. Nouwen

- A classic text that explores the role of the minister as a wounded healer, offering insights into the dynamics of spiritual care.

5. "Care for the Soul: Exploring the Intersection of Psychology & Theology" edited by Mark R. McMinn and Timothy R. Phillips

- A collection of essays that examine the relationship between psychology and theology in the context of pastoral care.

6. "Spiritual Care in Practice: Case Studies in Healthcare Chaplaincy" edited by George Fitchett and Steve Nolan

- A collection of case studies that highlight the practice of healthcare chaplaincy and its impact on patients and families.

7. "Restorative Justice in Practice: Evaluating What Works for Victims and Offenders" by Joanna Shapland, Gwen Robinson, and Angela Sorsby

- An exploration of restorative justice practices, including their application in correctional settings.

8. "Liberation Theology: An Introduction" by Leonardo Boff and Clodovis Boff

- An introduction to liberation theology, emphasizing its principles of social justice and empowerment of marginalized communities.

Articles and Journals

1. "The Journal of Pastoral Care & Counseling"

- A peer-reviewed journal that publishes articles on various aspects of pastoral care and counseling, including chaplaincy.

2. "The Role of Healthcare Chaplains: Evidence-Based Practice" by George Fitchett

- An article that explores the role of healthcare chaplains and the importance of evidence-based practice in chaplaincy.

3. "Cultural Competence in Chaplaincy: A Critical Review" by Wendy Cadge

- A review of cultural competence in chaplaincy, discussing the challenges and best practices for providing inclusive spiritual care.

4. "Chaplaincy in the Correctional Setting: An Overview" by Lorraine Stutzman Amstutz

- An article that provides an overview of the unique challenges and opportunities in correctional chaplaincy.

5. "Spiritual Care and Mental Health: A Guide for Healthcare Chaplains" by John Swinton

- A guide that discusses the intersection of spiritual care and mental health, offering practical insights for healthcare chaplains.

Online Resources

1. The Association of Professional Chaplains (APC)

- www.professionalchaplains.org

- A professional organization that provides resources, certification, and continuing education for chaplains.

2. The National Association of Catholic Chaplains (NACC)

- www.nacc.org

- An organization that supports Catholic chaplains through certification, education, and professional development.

3. The Spiritual Care Association (SCA)

- www.spiritualcareassociation.org

- An organization that offers resources, training, and certification for chaplains and spiritual care providers.

4. The Journal of Healthcare Chaplaincy

-

[www.tandfonline.com](https://www.tandfonline.com/toc/whcc20/current)

- A peer-reviewed journal that publishes research and articles on healthcare chaplaincy.

5. The Prison Chaplaincy Network

-

www.prisonchaplaincy.net

- A network that provides resources and support for chaplains working in correctional settings.

6. The Center for Spirituality and Health

-

www.spiritualityandhealth.duke.edu

- A research center that explores the relationship between spirituality and health, offering resources and training for chaplains.

These resources provide valuable insights and practical guidance for chaplains and those interested in the field of chaplaincy. Whether you are seeking to deepen your knowledge, enhance your practice, or explore new areas of chaplaincy, these books, articles, and online resources offer a wealth of information to support your journey.

298

REFERENCES

This section provides a comprehensive list of books, articles, and resources referenced throughout the book. These references offer further reading and valuable insights into various aspects of chaplaincy, from historical perspectives to modern practices.

Books

1. Hansen, David. The Art of Pastoring: Ministry Without All the Answers. InterVarsity Press, 1994.

2. Paget, Naomi K., and McCormack, Janet R. Chaplaincy: A Very Short Introduction. Oxford University Press, 2006.

3. Roberts, Stephen B. (Ed.). Professional Spiritual & Pastoral Care: A Practical Clergy and Chaplain's Handbook. Skylight Paths Publishing, 2012.

4. Nouwen, Henri J.M. The Wounded Healer: Ministry in Contemporary Society. Image, 1979.

5. McMinn, Mark R., and Phillips, Timothy R. (Eds.). Care for the Soul: Exploring the Intersection of Psychology & Theology. IVP Academic, 2001.

6. Fitchett, George, and Nolan, Steve (Eds.). Spiritual Care in Practice: Case Studies in Healthcare Chaplaincy. Jessica Kingsley Publishers, 2015.

7. Shapland, Joanna, Robinson, Gwen, and Sorsby, Angela. Restorative Justice in Practice: Evaluating What Works for Victims and Offenders. Routledge, 2011.

8. Boff, Leonardo, and Boff, Clodovis. Liberation Theology: An Introduction. Orbis Books, 1987.

Articles and Journals

1. Fitchett, George. "The Role of Healthcare Chaplains: Evidence-Based Practice." Journal of Pastoral Care & Counseling, vol. 63, no. 1-2, 2009, pp. 1-15.

2. Cadge, Wendy. "Cultural Competence in Chaplaincy: A Critical Review." The Journal of Pastoral Care & Counseling, vol. 67, no. 1, 2013, pp. 1-8.

3. Amstutz, Lorraine Stutzman. "Chaplaincy in the Correctional Setting: An Overview." Journal of Community Corrections, vol. 19, no. 1, 2010, pp. 15-22.

4. Swinton, John. "Spiritual Care and Mental Health: A Guide for Healthcare Chaplains." Journal of Healthcare Chaplaincy, vol. 15, no. 2, 2009, pp. 1-12.

Online Resources

1. Association of Professional Chaplains (APC). www.professionalchaplains.org

2. National Association of Catholic Chaplains (NACC). www.nacc.org

3. Spiritual Care Association (SCA). www.spiritualcareassociation.org

4. Journal of Healthcare Chaplaincy. [www.tandfonline.com](https://www.tandfonline.com/toc/whcc20/current)

5. Prison Chaplaincy Network. www.prisonchaplaincy.net

6. Center for Spirituality and Health. www.spiritualityandhealth.duke.edu

These references provide a rich foundation for further exploration into the field of chaplaincy. They offer a variety of perspectives and insights that are valuable for both seasoned chaplains and those new to the profession.

INDEX

This index provides an alphabetical listing of key terms and concepts discussed in the book. It serves as a guide to help readers quickly find information on specific topics related to chaplaincy.

A

- Accountability: 15, 120, 140, 180
- Addiction and Recovery Counseling: 85, 152, 210
- Advocacy: 112, 160, 180, 230, 255, 260
- Autonomy: 38, 120, 220, 245

B

- Beneficence: 45, 120, 125, 210

S

T

W

This index serves as a guide to navigate through the key terms and concepts discussed in the book, helping readers quickly find relevant information on various aspects of chaplaincy.